"Jennie and Levi aren't just wonderful pastors (or some of our best friends)—they're the kind of people who put in the hard work, dig deep, and fight for their marriage. Whether you've been married for two years or twenty, this book will help you strengthen your relationship and your faith."

—STEVEN AND HOLLY FURTICK

"We love Levi and Jennie! They are great people, great friends, and most importantly, having a great impact for Jesus! *The Marriage Devotional* is for all who want to experience more in their marriage! More meaning, more purpose, more fun, more intimacy! The Luskos give us an inside look at the 'best and worst' of what they've experienced in marriage so far. It's humble, honest, and honoring. We've learned a lot from them, and we hope by reading this, you will too!"

—TIM AND DEMI-LEIGH TEBOW

"There is nothing better than living inside of God's design, especially when it comes to marriage. From the beginning of this devotional to the end, the Luskos engage you in an honest and thought-provoking journey as they both aim to strengthen, sharpen, and remind you of all God created marriage to be. Who better to learn from than the Luskos? Not only is this an incredible read that was truly hard to put down, but it will be a resource we will be going back to often."

—CHRISTIAN AND SADIE HUFF

"This raw and real devotional offers hard-won wisdom, reminding us our good/hard relationships are so worth fighting for."

— JAY AND KATHERINE WOLF

"We are so excited about this amazing book on marriage by Jennie and Levi. Their story is an incredible example of a strong Christian marriage that is thriving through the highs and lows in life. Because of their experiences this devotional has thoughtful insights for every stage of marriage. The prayers and tips at the end of each chapter will give you practical ways to bring God into your marriage and help your relationship grow stronger than you ever imagined. We are so thankful for this resource and trust it blesses you like it did us."

— SHANE AND ROBBIE KIMBROUGH

"Whether you are newly married or decades in, there is wisdom in this book for you. Levi and Jennie address the good, the hard, and the real-life nitty-gritty—a place many books don't dare to venture! This isn't a stale book of dos and don'ts; it's a manual filled with practical tips, conversation starters, and biblical wisdom to set you on the path to the thriving marriage God has for you."

— BOB AND MARIA GOFF

"An encouraging and thought-provoking book, more than self-help. We believe if you take this seriously and honestly answer the questions put forward by Levi and Jennie, you will see breakthrough in your marriage."

— BEN AND TAYA GAUKRODGER

THE
MARRIAGE
DEVOTIONAL

THE MARRIAGE DEVOTIONAL

52 DAYS TO STRENGTHEN THE SOUL OF YOUR MARRIAGE

LEVI AND JENNIE LUSKO

W PUBLISHING GROUP

AN IMPRINT OF THOMAS NELSON

Published in Nashville, Tennessee, by W Publishing, an imprint of Thomas Nelson.

The authors are represented by Wolgemuth & Associates. www.wolgemuthandassociates.com

Thomas Nelson titles may be purchased in bulk for educational, business, fundraising, or sales promotional use. For information, please email SpecialMarkets@ThomasNelson.com.

ISBN 978-0-7852-9137-4 (HC)
ISBN 978-0-7852-9139-8 (eBook)
ISBN 978-0-7852-9140-4 (audiobook)
ISBN 978-0-7852-9138-1 (TP)

Library of Congress Control Number: 2022940283

Printed in the United States of America

24 25 26 27 28 LBC 5 4 3 2 1

Dedicated to the olive plants around our table.
May the soul of your parent's marriage be a
blessing to your children's children.

—PSALM 128:3

CONTENTS

PART 4: LET'S TALK ABOUT SEX AND FUN AND A SEXY, FUN MARRIAGE

PART 5: REGRETS, BAGGAGE, AND OTHER UNNECESSARY, HEAVY THINGS

PART 6: PRIDE SEPARATES US FROM GOD, AND HUMILITY DRAWS US CLOSER TO HIM

PART 7: THERE'S ALWAYS ROOM TO GROW IN COMMUNICATION

PART 8: HEALTH AND SOUL HYGIENE

PART 9: OBEDIENCE AND SUBMISSION ARE MORE AWESOME THAN YOU MIGHT THINK

PART 10: THE ART OF VALUING AND CELEBRATING

PART 11: UNLEASH THE BLESSINGS

PART 12: FINDING THE WAY FORWARD

INTRODUCTION

LEVI

In August 2018, Jennie and I were scheduled to preach in Chicago, and we tacked on an extra day to enjoy the city and spend some time together before we were due to speak. It was summer, and Chicago was hot, so we decided to rent bikes and go for a ride around the city.

At first it was perfect—we went by Millennium Park and headed toward the water. The beautiful Lakefront Trail that runs along Lake Michigan includes a bike path, and we headed toward Doane Observatory at the Adler Planetarium. This trail is gorgeous, but on this particular stretch it is a little sketchy. The path slants somewhat toward the water and drops off into the lake, and any waves cause the water to splash on the cement a little bit or a lot depending on the wind—and since it's the Windy City, you can count on some wet pavement. There were bright-yellow signs painted on the ground that said Slippery When Wet, urging caution to those riding on that side of the path.

At some point our romantic outing kind of devolved. Jennie and I got into a fight—which was frustrating because this was supposed to be our perfect day to ourselves. It wasn't a convenient time for relational disharmony. I don't even remember what the fight was about, but as we biked against the Chicago sky-line, I ended up saying something that didn't sit well with her. It was probably something to the effect of, "Why couldn't you have picked a better day to get your feelings hurt?"

Jennie accelerated to get ahead of me and create some space between us. I saw that she picked a bad time to accelerate, as we were heading into a curve. I called out, "Watch out! Slow down!" But she couldn't hear me—or more likely, because she was mad she *pretended* she couldn't hear me—and instead of slowing down, she pedaled faster. Her wheels touched the water just as she entered the turn, and she went down. Hard.

I rode up, and as soon as I ascertained that the only thing injured was her pride, I made the foot-in-mouth decision of pointing out that she had just ridden past approximately twenty Slippery When Wet signs in her own personal Tour de France rampage. Note to self: this was not helpful. It took her anger in the moment to Hulk status. We had an icy, silent ride back to return the bikes before we were emotionally able to work through the conflict and get back to a good spot.

Only looking back can we see the humor of the moment and how ridiculous it all was.

JENNIE

This is all too true, and honestly, not a reaction I easily admit to, because I was in a moooood. And when the storm clouds came in that day, they came in *strong*. Something I've learned about myself over the years is that I tend to run away from conflict. If things aren't going well between me and someone, whether it's Levi or anyone else, I tend to withdraw and not stick around. So this was a classic Jennie moment (before I learned some tools for fighting fair and staying present in said fight). But hey, that was a real moment for us! And I'm guessing that might be something you and your spouse have experienced, too, if you're humans and married and want to have a great marriage.

We were talking recently about how our Chicago bike story is a perfect metaphor for relationships. The sign that alerts the pedestrian or skateboarder or angry bike rider in a fight with her husband—Slippery When Wet—is a good warning on the road, and it's especially appropriate for marriage. The surface of our relationship can change from day to day. When we face storms, the path that was fine when we'd last pedaled down it is now slippery because it's wet. We might start to slip, and we might even fall hard. But there's strength in getting up, moving through, continuing forward, and navigating ahead with the resources and tools available to us. As we pay attention to the signs and wisdom around us, it's possible for us to adjust our speed and begin to make headway. At times we might go slower than we think we should be going, and we might have to stop at points and reconfigure.

That's why Levi and I decided to write *The Marriage Devotional*. We'll talk about this slippery road of marriage comprehensively, honestly, and with eyes toward the wisdom God makes available to us. In the midst of the unknown roads, He paves a solid path for us. He gives clear instructions along the way, and He's generous with grace and strength and vision when we make a mess of things. He also has a breathtaking design and destination for us as we move forward together. Marriage was His idea, after all.

You two might have a great marriage, so this devotional is something that will hopefully encourage you and help you fine-tune and deepen your relationship. Or you might be in a place where you think a great, godly, fun marriage seems like a lofty, far-off, hard-to-attain thing. We hope we can help you navigate these waters. We have a different story than you, but we've been in hard places in our relationship. We don't presume to know it all, but we do know where we've been and what God has taught us on the journey.

If all goes well, we won't end up perfect people in perfect relationship with each other, because that's not realistic or possible or even the goal. Rather, our aim is to create a space for you as a couple to connect, to talk through various subjects—the hard, the good, the helpful, the fun—that can bring depth to your relationship with Jesus and your spouse, and ultimately bring glory to God.

We believe it's possible in marriage to feel the wind in our hair as we look over at each other, smiling, riding in tandem. There is the potential for your marriage to be exhilarating and inspiring—but it takes work. We want to talk about this potential and the powerful relationship you two were meant to live out together.

LEVI

The original title of this book was going to be *Slippery When Wet*. Jennie and I came across another sign with those words stenciled on it on a different bike ride when we started working on this book and were brainstorming ideas for the title, and seeing the sign reminded us of that rough day in Chicago. Fortunately, this time the relationship vibe was romantic and fun, and as we imagined those words on the cover, we were like "Boom, done!" We laughed about telling that story right out of the gate because it's real life and would set the tone for a relatable reading experience.

But it turns out that when you google *slippery when wet*, it takes you to places in the dark corners of the internet that are *not* the website for this devotional. And when we relayed the idea to our publisher and they googled it, they ran for the Tums. (Tossing my publisher curveballs like this probably shouldn't give me as much pleasure as it does. I still remember when I said I wanted the back of my book *Swipe Right* to say in all caps, "GOD WANTS YOU TO HAVE AMAZING SEX," I heard an audible gasp over the phone. Oddly satisfying.) They protested that *Slippery When Wet* would come across as crass and offend prudish sensibilities. In our opinion that title would cut through the noise and set the tone for realizing that what you hold in your hands is a different take on a subject that badly needs a fresh perspective.

Jennie is all too right about the road of marriage being slippery in a bad way. But it also occurred to us that, on another level, we want our relationships to stay slippery. Think about it: When an engine seizes, it's because it's not lubricated. Stop changing your oil and watch what happens to your vehicle after a while. Hint: it won't work. And when we have God's grace and love and the Holy Spirit (which is symbolized as oil in the Bible) coating our relationships, and we're steady in God's Word, we can be slippery in a good way. We're not going to stick to conflicts. We're not going to stick to the wounds that come from living in close quarters every day. We're not going to stick to our past mistakes or our worst moments.

In a marriage, staying slippery is a powerful thing. And yes, it does present an amazing sexual double entendre. In this devotional we will get real about sex, which is a beautiful part of marriage. The best defense is a good offense, and if you don't want to end up having sex with someone you aren't married to, then you ought to have tons of sex with the person you *are* married to. Stay slippery, friends. (This isn't your grandma's marriage devo, but she's welcome to read it too. Go, Grandma, go!)

In the end Jennie and I fell in love with the concept of the book being titled *The Marriage Devotional*. We're going to talk about all of it and the incredible purpose God has for us as we move forward. This book is geared for all situations and all seasons in marriage, slippery in all ways.

JENNIE

Honestly, if you've picked up this book as a couple, we feel a kinship with you. You're our kind of people. If we saw you guys fighting on the bike trail, we would look at each other and go, "Yep. Godspeed, dear comrades." We think you're going to have plenty of "Oh yes, that's us" moments together in the coming weeks (at least we hope we're not alone in our issues!) and uncover a lot of amazing opportunities to get your relationship sliding along in a good way.

So in that spirit, Levi and I are going to take turns sharing the best and worst of what we've encountered on our path of marriage so far. We'll encourage you the best we can and draw from the Bible for wisdom and truth and some seriously helpful directional signs. We'll offer some ways to connect to each other and have the kind of real talks that can cause flourishing in a marriage. And most importantly, we'll offer ways for you to connect with God, together and separately, and explore what He has for us as married people.

Of course we're going to have some fun along the way, because hey, we're the Luskos (wink, wink)! We deeply believe that God wants the two of you to have a fun, fresh, strong, powerful, thriving, and growing relationship—not only one that will make your time on this earth blessed but also one that God will use to bless the world. It's real. It's powerful. And you can be a part of it as your marriage thrives.

So come with us on this sometimes slippery, often beautiful road. Bring your helmets (for safety) and your hearts to receive what God has for you, and we believe we'll end up somewhere amazing together.

MARRIAGE HAS A PURPOSE

LOVE NOTES

The LORD, before whom I have walked faithfully, will send his angel with you and make your journey a success, so that you can get a wife for my son from my own clan and from my father's family.

GENESIS 24:40

CHAPTER 1

RIGHT PLACE, RIGHT TIME

JENNIE

L evi and I were close to becoming brother- and sister-in-law. I know, it's shocking, and it was weird to say for a long time, but now it's just funny. I was dating someone, and he was dating someone, and they happened to be brother and sister. It wasn't like we were engaged and they were engaged—but it was serious enough that we thought we might get married to these people we were dating. Then . . . plot twist . . . Jennie meets Levi. Levi meets Jennie. The rest is history.

I think of the situation almost like a dollhouse, where a kid puts all the people in different rooms—one in the kitchen, one sitting by the fireplace, one upside down in the bathroom—when God shows up and says, "Oh, what are you doing here, little one? You need to go *here*. I need to take you over there. And Jennie, I will move you to Albuquerque, New Mexico, etc." He takes His hand, reaches in, and starts moving things around in the way only He can, in *His* time and in *His* plan.

When Levi and I look back, it's just so funny to us that we were that close to becoming in-laws. Funny like creepy and weird, yes—but also hilarious. Mostly, though, we can see how God is in control and knows exactly what He's doing. It's mostly an issue of aligning our hearts with His in the journey He sets out for us.

So often we think we know the plan for how things need to happen and when. We say things like, "This is how my life is going to go. These are my people, this is my purpose, and this is my plan." But in all honesty, do we really know? How can we know His thoughts or His ways or His timing? God literally said it perfectly in Isaiah 55:8–9:

> "For my thoughts are not your thoughts,
>   neither are your ways my ways,"
> declares the LORD.
> "As the heavens are higher than the earth,
>   so are my ways higher than your ways,
>   and my thoughts than your thoughts."

God knows, and He is in control. If we can just surrender—and keep surrendering—to Him and His thoughts and ways, He will bring the right things and people, in the right place, at the right time. Proverbs 16:9 says, "In their hearts humans plan their course, but the LORD establishes their steps." And goodness, am I thankful He does. We have a part in planning, but we also have a part in surrendering to God's greatest plan for us.

No matter what happens, we are meant to lift our eyes to God, depend on Him, and trust in Him. He's calling us to a life of faith. A life in Christ. We can trust Him on the unknown road before us. We don't know what our future holds, but we know the One who holds the future (to paraphrase Corrie ten Boom).[1] God sees both our past and our future from His vantage point, and He has a plan: and our marriage is included in this plan.

To bring us back to today's Bible verse: God "will send his angel with you and make your journey a success." The *you* in the text refers to Abraham's servant, and Abraham was giving him a pep talk. The servant was about to leave on an all-important journey to find a wife for Abraham's son, Isaac. God's angel led

REMEMBERING REQUIRES LOOKING BACK.

REMEMBER HOW GOD HAS BEEN FAITHFUL TO YOU.

THERE'S NO BETTER WAY TO BUILD YOUR FAITH FOR THE FUTURE OF YOUR MARRIAGE.

the servant on a roundabout journey to find the right girl. Rebekah "just happened" to be visiting the well at the same time the servant had asked for a sign, and it turned out she was exactly the one he'd been looking for. The marriage of Isaac and Rebekah was stunning. (You can read about it starting in Genesis 24, if you're up for a swoon.) God set all this up. He moved them around and brought them together—in His perfect will. And while this story is specific to them, I believe God wants all of us to have a journey of success within our relationships with our spouses.

How were you and your spouse set up? What's your relationship story? Do you believe you were brought together by God? There's no better way to build your faith for the future of your marriage than by looking back and remembering how God has been faithful to you. Even if you didn't know Him, you can still see His fingerprints.

You can trust Him. He moved the dolls in your house to just the right spot. You two were at the right place at the right time, and now you're together—and here's the thing: God has so much more in store for you as you both keep choosing to show up. And one thing is for certain, it is going to be good.

BRING IT HOME

- Trace back through the period of time before you two were brought together. What moves did God make to put you in each other's path? What people or situations did He rearrange to bring you into a serious relationship?
- Which of those moves were happy and fun at the time? Which of them felt terrible but led to good ultimately?

- How would you describe your trust level with God right now? Knowing that He has brought you two this far, how does it make you feel to know that He will also be with you on the potentially hazardous and slippery road ahead?

CONVERSATION STARTERS

- "Looking back to our early days, I'm so glad we stuck together when _____, and we could have split. What was God doing in our hearts in those days?"
- "In my story with you, I think God's smallest move to rearrange people in the dollhouse with the biggest impact was _____."
- "Considering things we'd wished we'd known back then, a simple way we can keep looking to God to follow His moves going forward might be _____."

PRAYER

God, we remember right now that You have been faithful to us. Thank You for bringing us together at the right time and the right place, according to Your perfect plan. We celebrate what You have done in our hearts in the past, and now we commit to trust You and look to You as You continue to work in us. In Jesus' name, amen.

They are no longer two, but one flesh.
Therefore what God has joined together,
let no one separate.

MATTHEW 19:6

CHAPTER 2

GOD CARES ABOUT MARRIAGE

LEVI

I had to fix a flat tire on my electric bike the other day, so I needed to go to the company's website to figure out, *How do I get this tire (which also houses the motor) off? How do I first disengage the disc brake? And how do I get it all back on and not have it come apart when I am going down the road at twenty-eight miles an hour?* When I finally got Humpty-Dumpty back together again, to my eternal frustration, the tire was wobbling. But I didn't want to take it to a bike store. Ain't nobody got time for that. So I googled *How do you fix wobble in tire?* and wouldn't you know . . . there's a video for that on YouTube.

Sometimes our marriages can wobble, too, and we've got to turn somewhere for help. There are many options but, as far as I am concerned, only one good choice. The B-I-B-L-E. (That's the book for me.) I am so thankful that God wrote a book. And He has a whole lot to say about marriage. He doesn't want your relationship to wobble, or go flat, or for your brakes to squeak. He wants to save you the relational heartache of flying over the handlebars or ending up stranded by the side of the road picking bits of asphalt out of your road rash.

God, who made the world, wrote to you about marriage. He hasn't left you scrambling without instructions. He cares about marriage. He invented it! He gave marriage to us as a gift. It's a blessing, and it's from Him. Let's keep that in mind as we talk about marriage. God made it; therefore, He should be the One to tell us how to use it. And since it's God-given, it should be God-governed.

Scripture's teaching on marriage is that you and your spouse are supposed to *complement* each other, not *complete* each other or *compete* with each other. You weren't half a person before you got married, and your spouse doesn't make you whole. They are not your opponent; they are your teammate and your partner.

Because of relationships we see in movies, we can find ourselves thinking the opposite is true: *When I meet the person of my dreams, that person is going to complete me, and everything will just be dreamy.* However, we quickly learn that even the most amazing, successful, good-looking, and Christlike spouse can't fill every weakness or meet every need in our lives. No person is capable of that.

I don't have the equipment, wherewithal, or hardware to complete Jennie. She has to find that in God. When she does, I can complement her; I'm going to be strong in some areas where she's weak (and vice versa).

But when we make the mistake of expecting our spouses to complete us, we put a huge burden on them. And, hey, marriage is already hard without those kinds of expectations. Life is hard. It's challenging. We are basically two sinners living together in close proximity all the time. That other person *never goes away*. It has the makings of a cage match. If we're not approaching each other with the right spirit, we'll start looking to our spouses to do something only God can do.

If you came into marriage with expectations that your spouse would be your savior, who would complete you and fix you, know that God will lead you away from that misguided belief if you ask Him. That's a lot of pressure to put on any human—but God can take it. He *wants* to take it. He says, "Come to Me with your neediness, then let Me guide you in making your marriage beautiful. Love Me. Respect Me. And then give to your spouse from the overflow I give you." Only God's shoulders can handle the weight of your soul.

Genesis 1:27 tells us that God made men and women "in his own image" to crave relationship and thrive in relationship. God's purpose for marriage goes all the way back to Adam and Eve, when He created it. Genesis 2:22 says, "the LORD God made a woman from the rib he had taken out of the man, and he brought her to the man." And in today's verse we see that when God joins a man and woman in marriage, "they are no longer two, but one flesh." God brought the first two people together in marriage so they could have a complementary relationship—and so He could launch an epic rescue operation through it. Clearly God cares about marriage. And He cares about yours.

BRING IT HOME

- Why is it easy to forget that God cares about marriage? What does considering this simple fact reveal to you about your relationship with your spouse?
- Have you ever subscribed to the "you complete me" idea of marriage? Is that something you've believed in the past, or have you ever found yourself acting that way? How did that happen?
- What's the difference between complementing and completing each other—both in general and for you and your spouse? How does God make it possible for you and your spouse to complement each other rather than trying to complete each other?

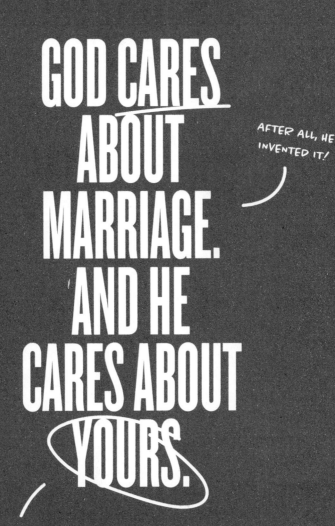

GOD WAS THERE

- Together list some of your marriage milestones—big events, accomplishments, ups and downs, and turning points. You can think in terms of eras—in the past season, year, or however far back you two go.
- For each marriage milestone, go back and acknowledge that God was there, that it was just as big a deal for Him. God cares about each and every facet of your relationship! He celebrates these things with you, and He is also with you in the tears—every part of it. How does remembering God's presence in your marriage change the way you store these milestones in your hearts?

PRAYER

Father God, the simple fact that You care about marriage changes everything. And You not only care but You are also the answer to our every need and struggle. You empower us to do the impossible. Together we choose to submit to You, and we choose to follow Your plan for us. Show us how You alone complete us and how we complement each other in a unique and beautiful way. In Jesus' name, amen.

A man leaves his father and mother and is united with his wife, and they become one flesh.

GENESIS 2:24

CHAPTER 3

MARRIAGE: THE ROLE OF A LIFETIME

LEVI AND JENNIE

O ne of the trickiest parts of marriage is figuring out what roles you're going to play in your daily lives together—who is responsible for what, who takes the lead on what. It's a lifetime project. But one thing we don't have to be confused about is the role of marriage in the world as God meant it. Your role as husband and wife together is significant, and the Bible tells us a lot about its key components.

First, as today's verse tells us, your role together in marriage is to be *united.*

Think for a moment about the word *unity.* In Hebrew, to be united means "to designate exclusively or to concentrate fully."[1] So being united as husband and wife is coming together— exclusively—with no one else in the mix. It's an exclusive, set-apart relationship. It's a concentrated effort.

In our home we talk about being on the same team. When we're arguing or have an issue, we remind each other: "Same team." That's unity. Or to put it another way, we are on the same ship. This is not like the game Battleship, where we're trying to sink each other's ship and destroy each other. We are on the *same* ship, a relation*ship* of doing life together and fighting forward together.

The unity of marriage is also demonstrated in the sexual unity of husband and wife. Today's verse says that the two of them "become one flesh." This tells us that sex inside of marriage is a beautiful gift. It's saying, "I give myself completely and exclusively to you. I belong completely and exclusively to you. I am united with you."

And this sexual love ought to be enriching. After a while, as the excitement of newness fades, this intimate love is meant to grow. Sex is meant to be enjoyed in a man and woman's exclusive relationship for their lifetimes. There's such a beauty of growing in that. Sexual intimacy with your spouse should be enriching, and it should be all about giving, not taking.

So first, your role together as a married couple is to be united. Second, your role is to be *vulnerable*.

Genesis 2:25 tells us that Adam and Eve "were both naked, and they felt no shame." God's original design for us was to walk naked and unashamed—being fully open, fully vulnerable, fully intimate with each other. Can you imagine being in a place with your spouse where there's no shame or guilt? Just walking naked with your spouse in a beautiful garden God designed? That's literally what we were meant to do. To walk together with God. Everything open and out. Nothing hidden. Nothing secret. Nothing shameful. Enjoying that intimacy with God and with our spouse.

Vulnerability is the key to intimacy. Imagine your marriage as a place where you can share everything—your dreams, what matters to you, all that is in your heart. A safe place to invite your spouse to share their dreams, their heart, and where they are in life. A space where you both feel the freedom to ask hard questions and reveal deep parts of yourself. To know and feel known in the truest way. That is intimacy.

Third, along with being united and being vulnerable, the role of marriage is to be an *example* to the world.

Our ultimate role as a married couple is to show the world a beautiful picture of Jesus and the church—a loving, intimate, united relationship (Ephesians 5:25–33). When I think about the

VULNERABILITY IS THE KEY TO INTIMACY.

NOTHING HIDDEN, NOTHING SHAMEFUL, NOTHING SECRET

TO KNOW AND FEEL KNOWN IN THE TRUEST WAY

people in our church, I immediately think of some incredible married couples who give us a beautiful picture of Jesus and the church. They're not perfect. They have issues. But the way they love each other, work through things together, and honor each other is so beautiful. It's inspiring, and it fills everyone who watches them with hope. And that is part of the purpose of marriage.

Your marriage points to the greater marriage that's going to happen in the future, when Jesus will marry His bride, the church. And as Christians, that's who we are. We're His bride. The Bible tells us about the wedding supper of the Lamb, where we will get to celebrate and be with Jesus forever (Revelation 19:6–9). We'll get to be with Him face-to-face. There will be no more saying goodbye. There will be no more death, sorrow, or sadness. There will be only celebration for the rest of our lives in heaven, together, because of Jesus. It will be the best wedding imaginable!

In the meantime here on earth, we get to see marriages restored—through Jesus and through the church. We get to see marriages strengthened, and we celebrate people meeting each other and getting married. Over and over again, marriages show us new things about Jesus. So until He comes again, our roles and privilege in marriage are meant to involve being united, vulnerable, and a living example of what it is to be loved by God. And it's the role of a lifetime.

BRING IT HOME

- How might the idea of being on the same ship—not separate battleships—change the way you and your spouse have disagreements?

- Think about the idea of your sexual union in marriage growing, deepening, maturing, and enriching over time as you give to each other. What might you do to ensure things are going in this direction?
- What do you think about the idea of marriage being an example of Jesus' love for the church, His bride? What does this kind of love look like in your marriage? In what ways could you grow in this?

OPERATION VULNERABLE

- Plan a date night where you do an activity neither of you have ever done before—one that comes with a learning curve. It might be some kind of dance or sports class, or something crafty or creative.
- As (or after) you try the new thing and mess up, talk about what it means to be imperfect and vulnerable, and discuss the kinds of things that make you feel that way.
- Observe how you try to protect yourself in new or uncomfortable situations, and then relax in the company of the person you can be vulnerable and real with.

PRAYER

Father, show us how to pursue You more as a couple. There is a bigger picture of Your design for marriage in unity, vulnerability, and loving relationship with You. We say yes to the role You designed for our marriage to show the world Your love. In Jesus' name, amen.

Those who seek me find me.

PROVERBS 8:17

CHAPTER 4

PRACTICE HIS PRESENCE

LEVI AND JENNIE

D id you know we unlock our phones on average 150 times a day?[1] We tap, swipe, and click on our phones 2,617 times per day.[2] That's more times of touching our phones per 24 hours than there are minutes. You probably just did it, didn't you? Busted. (Well, hey, at least you know you're not alone.) That is a lot of looking down.

What if, instead, you got into the habit of looking up? How good would it be for your heart if 150 times a day you acknowledged God's presence and smiled at Him in your soul? What if 2,617 times a day you whispered an invitation for Him to open your eyes to see how He wants to use you at work or at school and gave Him a seat at the table in your finances and hobbies, or even in your loneliness? And what if you acknowledged that He is always right there with you, no matter what you are going through in your marriage?

When you acknowledge God's presence in your life and in your marriage, you turn the key in your spiritual ignition. His presence is a benefit to you most when you remember it, cultivate it, and lean into it. A command that's frequently repeated in Scripture is "Remember," because it is so easy to forget.

So try saying to God each morning, "I know You are here. I know You are with us." Say it when you are afraid or tempted. Say it when you are angry or disappointed. Let it become your release valve when you are ashamed. Run *to* Him, not *from* Him; remembering God's presence will help alter your story.

There is no limit to where you can take this because God will fill whatever space you create. Like the ocean that floods into the hole on the beach you dug between tides as a kid, He will fill any place in your life that you open up and make available to Him. Even if it's small. There is nothing too little, too big, too embarrassing, or too persistent that He can't turn around in your marriage once you open it up to Him.

There's an old hymn by Oliver Holden that will give you a brand-new way of looking at what is all around you:

> They who seek the throne of grace,
> Find that throne in every place;
> If we live a life of prayer,
> God is present everywhere.
>
> In our sickness or our health,
> In our want or in our wealth,
> If we look to God in prayer,
> God is present everywhere.[3]

God's with-you-ness in your life is even more unbreakable than wedding vows—for richer, for poorer; in sickness and in health. But just as you opened your heart to your spouse, and maybe one of you got down on one knee, you have to invite God into your life and your marriage. Interestingly enough, even though God is omnipresent, there is one place He won't invade unless invited—the human heart. "I stand at the door and knock," Jesus said. "If anyone hears my voice and opens the door, I will come in to him and eat with him, and he with me" (Revelation 3:20 ESV). To benefit from God's touch in your spirit, you must welcome Him in.

As you seek to rise up and live a life of strength and honor, nothing will give you greater peace and authority than embracing the power that comes from practicing the presence of God.

And remember, His presence in your life is not based on your performance. It's not like He's with you only on your good days. He's not more present in your marriage when you're getting along. He said, "*Never* will I leave you; *never* will I forsake you" (Hebrews 13:5). He is *always* with you, because that's who He is, not because of anything you have or haven't done. It doesn't matter what skeletons are in your closet—whether you were once addicted to drugs, or you've spent time behind bars, or your last marriage failed. The things behind you are no match for the One who is with you.

It can be easy to get stuck, to fixate on the bad things you have been through or done. It can be easy to focus on the hurt— that you weren't loved, that you're divorced, that you're an addict, that you're fatherless, or that you were sexually abused.

If you're not careful, lingering bitterness can turn into a victim mentality and a perpetually wounded spirit. You can let it control you and give you your name. But hear this: although it's easy to be defined by your dysfunction, it's not necessary.

The Greek word translated as *church* in the New Testament literally means "called-out ones."[4] Jesus loved you so much that He called you out of the crocodile-infested darkness and into His marvelous light. Royal blood was shed for you! You have been rescued, and your Rescuer is as close to you as you dare to acknowledge.

The more you practice His presence, the more you'll know His grace.

BRING IT HOME

- Since God fills the space you create for Him, how can the two of you create more space in your lives for Him on a daily basis?

THE THINGS BEHIND YOU ARE NO MATCH FOR THE ONE WHO IS WITH YOU.

"NEVER WILL I LEAVE YOU;
NEVER WILL I FORSAKE YOU."
HEBREWS 13:5

- In what areas would you dare to invite God into your marriage? Small ones? Big ones?
- In what ways have you been defined by the skeletons in your closet or dysfunction in your life? In your marriage? How is God calling you out of that?

REMINDERS

- Use your phones to start a new memory-habit of looking up. Set a new background screen, set some reminders, a recurring timer, or even stick something to your phone case to prompt you to recognize the presence of God. You can respond with something simple:
- I know You're with me.
- I invite You into _____.
- Thank You for being here.
- After you do this for a while, answer this: How does this change how your day goes?
- Send your spouse reminders of your presence in their life too. Send texts, voice memos, or pictures to remind each other throughout the day, "I'm thinking of you" or "Hey, you're hot and I love you."

PRAYER

God, thank You for pursuing us, for being closer to us than we know. We recognize that You will fill and renew every space we open up to You. We invite You into our marriage in a fresh way, and we will set our hearts to practice Your presence. In Jesus' name, amen.

PART 2

LET'S PUT SOME EFFORT IN OUR INTENTIONALITY

LOVE NOTES

Husbands, love your wives, just as Christ loved
the church and gave himself up for her.

EPHESIANS 5:25

CHAPTER 5

A MARRIAGE THAT WORKS

LEVI

A while back, I watched a *60 Minutes* interview with Steven Spielberg in which he said that he still got as worried, nervous, and scared about directing his twenty-seventh movie as he did on his first one. Isn't that amazing? The guy who made *Jaws*, *E.T.*, and the *Indiana Jones* movies still gets jittery on the job.[1]

Spielberg is arguably the most well-known and respected filmmaker in the world today. If anybody could just start phoning it in, it could be him. I mean, he could pretty much just sign his name on any screenplay and make it a guaranteed success. Yet every time this multi-award-winning director gets behind the camera, he approaches his craft as if it's his very first time and pours all his nervous excitement and energy into making that movie a success.

The same energy and focus that create a successful movie can also make a successful marriage. Whether your relationship is in its first year or twenty-seventh year, a solid marriage requires never phoning it in or going through the motions but rather taking your relationship seriously and applying yourself, heart and soul, day after day and year after year. Spielberg wouldn't be where he is today had he coasted. He would have slipped off the road into oblivion.

The truth is, marriages usually don't burn out; they rust out. It would be great if there were a class you could take or a pill you could swallow or a retreat you could go to that would be guaranteed to lead to a healthy, strong relationship, but there isn't. You just have to be willing to keep showing up and giving it your all and doing the hard things.

A successful marriage is spelled W-O-R-K. If your marriage isn't working right now, it might be because you aren't working at it. A strong relationship is not going to happen by itself. Too often we think passively when we should be thinking actively.

We sometimes talk about love as though it were an emotion, when it's really a verb. In today's verse the apostle Paul instructed husbands, "Love your wives." Notice that he was commanding an action, not describing a feeling. We hear people say stuff like, "I just fell out of love," or "I just don't love her anymore." But when you think of love as an active verb, both of those sound ridiculous. What would you say if I told you, "I just fell off my bike"? You'd probably tell me to get back on, and be careful on that slippery road. What if I said, "I just don't pay taxes anymore." You might give me a blank or confused stare. If you have "fallen out" of love or "just don't" love someone anymore, realize that obedience does not require feelings. Often when we do choose to obey, feelings develop.

It's like kindling a fire. Every summer, our family likes to go camping together. We sometimes pencil in our "Luskos in the wild" expeditions on our calendar months ahead of time. Other times I spontaneously declare, "Let's go camping this week!" After Jennie gives me the *"This week?! Okay, I can do that"* look, we're gearing up for adventures in the great outdoors. (By the way, planning vacations, romantic getaways, and even date nights protects these times from being just good intentions that get swallowed up by busyness. You'll never find time for the most important things in life; you must make time.)

Marriage must be approached the way you make a fire when camping: what takes only a spark to ignite requires diligent effort to maintain. Campfires don't flourish on their own, and left to

THE TRUTH IS:

GREAT MARRIAGES ARE MADE, NOT BORN.

A SUCCESSFUL MARRIAGE IS SPELLED W-O-R-K.

themselves, they will dwindle to ash. You must constantly add fuel to sustain a powerful fire.

Likewise, relationships are not self-sustaining or maintenance-free. Great marriages require a constant infusion of commitment, tears, and lots and lots of forgiveness. I also happen to agree with Dr. Dre, who once said, "Clear communication. Respect. A lot of laughter. And a lot of orgasms. That's what makes a marriage work."[2] Right on all points.

Having a great marriage is not easy. Very few things in this life that bring true joy are. What success can anyone find in any pursuit—academics, sports, work, music, science, literature—without putting in the effort and paying a price behind the scenes? Easy come, easy go. Great husbands and wives are made, not born.

BRING IT HOME

- What is the most important work you and your spouse are doing behind the scenes in your marriage? Where could you grow?
- How is it a relief to know that feelings go up and down but commitment and hard work bring rewards? How have you seen this in your relationship?
- What work are you two doing right now to "make" yourselves a great husband or wife?

CONVERSATION STARTERS

- "You may not think I notice, but I see how you _____ behind the scenes. This is what a difference it has made: _____."
- "I appreciate you and how you_____, and I love when you _____."

- "Sometimes I get a little passive about working on our marriage when _____."
- "Three active things we could do this week to work on our marriage are _____."

PRAYER

Father, You show us what hard work looks like in Your Word, such as how You created the heavens and the earth and how You came up with Your beautiful plan for our redemption through Jesus. You love creativity and design and things that require intention and hard work. You made relationships that way too. Thank You for what we have, and give us the love and strength to keep making decisions and doing the work of marriage well, so we can enjoy all that You have for us. In Jesus' name, amen.

Seek first [God's] kingdom and his righteousness, and all these things will be given to you as well.

MATTHEW 6:33

CHAPTER 6

BE THE ONE

JENNIE

When did you know your spouse was "the one"? Did you have some sort of earth-shaking revelation? Or did it slowly dawn on you? I want to talk about this concept of who "the one" is because it tends to get so much press.

Can I be honest here? (You're like, *Uh, yes—hopefully you've been honest this whole time!*) I never actually thought of Levi as "the one" before we got married. I remember one day, when we were dating, looking at him and thinking, *Man, I'd love to grow old with this guy.* I knew he was the man of my dreams—a man who loved Jesus more than anything, who loved serving Him with his life, and who was hilarious and fun. But I never had goose bumps or the audible voice of God tell me, "Dear Jennifer Michelle, this is the man you will marry. He is the one for you!" I just really liked Levi and loved him, and God intersected our lives and led us toward each other in a simple, yet powerful and obvious way.

Just to be clear, I now know and am confident in and *love* that Levi is indeed the one for me. I'm the lucky one!

But as romantic as it is, I think the concept of "the one" really limits us. So often we fixate on finding "the one" when we're single, and then we worry if we actually did find the right one after we've found them. When we find ourselves in the hard moments, struggles, and frustrations of marriage, we might think, *Oh gosh. I don't know if this person is actually the right one. Did I get it all wrong?* And we worry that we made a mistake. Then if things get slippery, that thought is in the back of our minds, and the marriage gets even wobblier. And we doubt when we should be pouring encouragement and grace and strength and faith over our struggles.

But the real question is not about whether the person you married is "the one." It's about whether *you* are the one. It's so much more important to focus on who *you* are, who *you* are becoming, and the issues in your own heart.

Pastor Andy Stanley likes to ask people who are looking for their mate, "Are you the person the person you're looking for is looking for?"[1] And even after we're married, it's still good to ask ourselves the same question—just in a different light. *Am I that person? Am I "the one"? Am I continuously becoming "the one" for my spouse?*

It can be easy to blame your spouse for their attitudes, actions, and failures. It can be easy to put the focus on them for not being the one God is calling them to be. But what if you looked inward more? What if you focused on who you are and who you are becoming as an individual? What would it look like to be more concerned with your own heart before God, asking Him to open your eyes to your own need for Him to move and work and finesse and fix?

I love how Psalm 139:23–24 (NKJV) leads us in a simple prayer with such thoughts backing it up:

> Search me, O God, and know my heart;
> Try me, and know my anxieties;
> And see if there is any wicked way in me,
> And lead me in the way everlasting.

Continually go to God and take responsibility for yourself (doing your part to be "the one" God is calling you to be). Then and only then can you rest in the work God is doing in your heart and also

GOD'S HEART FOR US, IN ALL OF LIFE, IS THAT WE WOULD PUT HIM FIRST AND SEEK HIM FIRST IN EVERYTHING.

SEE WHAT GOD CAN DO WITH A HEART THAT SEEKS HIM FIRST!

in your spouse's heart. He's your perfect Father, and He knows you best. You can rest in that fully.

Let's take another look at today's verse: "Seek first [God's] kingdom and His righteousness, and all these things will be given to you as well." Here Jesus talks specifically about clothing and food and shelter, but God's heart for us in all of life is that we would put Him first and seek Him first in everything. He wants to take care of all of the things we don't need to worry about—and He wants us to let Him.

Let's each make the decision to pray this "search me, O God, prayer." Let's see what God can do with a heart that seeks Him first above everything. Let's find out how God might want to impact our marriage as we look inward first before trying to point the finger.

BRING IT HOME

- Did you ever believe in the concept of finding "the one"? Has that belief or disbelief affected your journey toward marriage and your commitment to your spouse?
- Do you feel like you are becoming "the one" God made you to be? Are you getting closer? At a standstill? Going backward? Write down your thoughts.
- Do you truly believe that if you put God first, "all these things will be given to you as well" in your marriage? If so, how can you continue toward that goal? If not, what are your worries?

CONVERSATION STARTERS

- "When I look at you, I see you becoming the one God has called you to be in _____."

- "I see growth in your life in this area specifically: _____."
- "I would describe the kind of person I feel called to be as _____. How is my progress in getting there?"
- "I have felt God personally growing and changing me as an individual through the process of our marriage in this way: _____."

PRAYER

Lord, by Your Spirit, help us continue to grow and become "the one" for each other. Fashion us into the ones You've created us to be. Strengthen us to grow personally and to seek first Your kingdom and Your righteousness, so we can let go and let You be our Lord and Shepherd in our togetherness. You do all things well, and we trust You. In Jesus' name, amen.

Jesus said to the servants, "Fill the jars with water"; so they filled them to the brim. Then he told them, "Now draw some out and take it to the master of the banquet." They did so, and the master of the banquet tasted the water that had been turned into wine. He did not realize where it had come from, though the servants who had drawn the water knew. Then he called the bridegroom aside and said, ". . . You have saved the best till now."

JOHN 2:7–10

CHAPTER 7

TO THE BRIM

LEVI

Don't you want to laugh when you read about Jesus' miracle of turning water into wine? Imagine the maître d' tasting that wine and saying, "Wow! I thought we were all out . . . and this wine is fantastic." Then maybe he asked the servants, "What year is this?"

"Uh, year?" they might have responded.

"Yeah, what vintage is it?" he would have pressed. "Was it aged for years in oak barrels in Napa?"

"No," they would have clarified, "it was made like ten seconds ago in a stone bathtub by Jesus."

Talk about the world's most overqualified bartender. It would be like the president selling stamps in a post office. Ridiculousness aside, this miracle is significant because it is the first miracle Jesus performed in His public ministry. That makes a statement, doesn't it? When He was thirty, the Holy Spirit came upon Him at His baptism, and with all the power in the universe coursing through Him, He—wait for it—went to a wedding and solved a catering catastrophe.

What?

Aside from being plain delightful, this miracle tells us a couple of things. First, *relationships matter to God*. Jesus made an appearance at this couple's celebration of their love and responded to their needs. You'd think running out of wine would be a small detail, but He cared enough to provide that for them and sustain their joy (and because His mom asked).

But maybe the biggest lesson from this text is that we can

have as much from Jesus as we want. It all depends on how much we're willing to pour in. Let me explain.

Remember, the servants at this wedding couldn't flip on a faucet or turn on a hose. They had to go out to the well, pull up a bucket of water, carry it to the jar, and pour it out. To fill all six pots (that each carried twenty to thirty gallons) would have required going back again and again and again and again.

The text says the servants filled them "to the brim" (John 2:7). That is super impressive, because the servants had no guarantees this plan was going to work. To fill up these huge water jars even halfway still would have been backbreaking work. To fill them three-fourths full—intense. But they filled them *to the brim*. They didn't stop going to the well until there was no more room for water. The wedding guests received 120 to 180 gallons of wine, because that is how much water the servants poured in.

What does this have to do with relationships? So many people today live and operate with only enough in the tank to get by. The bare minimum. Running low is a way of life, like the 10 percent battery life remaining on my iPhone right now (which makes Jennie nervous) or her car's gas tank sitting at 10 percent full (which makes me nervous). Many people also flirt with the redline relationally. Their marriages are running on fumes, hanging on by a thread.

Living that way is cruising for a crash, because when you put in only what is required and no more, all it takes is one bad month, one bad fight, or one unforeseen crisis to push you beyond the point of no return.

Several years ago Jennie and I endured a marriage storm that, statistically speaking, should have done us in. When parents have to bury a child, the relationship often doesn't survive. And sadly,

WE CAN HAVE AS MUCH FROM JESUS AS WE WANT.

AND FROM MARRIAGE

IT ALL DEPENDS ON HOW MUCH WE'RE WILLING TO POUR IN.

we have seen that happen to other couples. We write this with all humility, giving all glory to God: our marriage, while not without its issues, is better and stronger today than it's ever been.

I have a hunch that a trial, such as a child's going to heaven, doesn't destroy the marriage; it just exposes the weakness of a marriage's foundation. It's like how pottery going into the furnace explodes hairline fractures. The beautiful thing about trials, though, is that they only amplify and enhance what goes in; while they can make a weak marriage weaker, they can also make a strong marriage stronger.

This is why it's critical that you and your spouse train for the trials you are not yet in. Barely enough is not good enough. We need to approach marriage with a to-the-brim mentality—because we are privileged to have a God who provides like that. Keep filling up your jars with intention, attention, and kindness, and know that He can miraculously transform your water into the finest vintage.

BRING IT HOME

- What is the scariest thing for you and your spouse to run low on? Gas? Phone charge? Toilet paper? Coffee? What might the things you stock up on and run out of a lot in your home say about what's important to you on a daily basis?
- When have you felt like you were running on fumes in your relationship? What were the circumstances? How did that "bare minimum" manifest itself in your interactions?
- How can you pour more into your relationship "jar" during good times that will help you when you're running low like that again?

DO A TASTING

Have you ever been to a wine tasting? What about a "coffee cup-ping" or tea ceremony? Check out something like this locally if it's offered, or look up online how to do one together. As you do, you might be surprised to learn the background of what goes into the water to make the magic: the plants that are nurtured, leaves and fruit that are carefully harvested, artisanal processing, dedication, craftsmanship, and time that creates the liquid you have in your cup. Learn to taste differences in quality and variety, and discover what you like most. After you enjoy that together, maybe your next sip at home will remind you of all that went into it—and what can come from pouring that kind of dedication into your marriage too.

PRAYER

Lord God, thank You for the way You take our watery efforts and turn them into something beautiful. We commit to keep bringing them to You and to each other, and to keep asking for Your blessing and power because You are faithful. Open our eyes to the places that need filling in our hearts individually and in our marriage. Have Your way in our lives, and pour out what You know we need in our marriage. In Jesus' name, amen.

The law was given through Moses; grace
and truth came through Jesus Christ.

JOHN 1:17

CHAPTER 8

GIVE MOSES A PINK SLIP

LEVI AND JENNIE

It's significant that Jesus' first miracle was turning water into wine at a wedding; He turned plain H_2O into a beverage that, in Scripture, is a symbol for medicine and celebration. But back in the Old Testament, Moses turned water into blood. When Moses told Pharaoh to release the Israelites from slavery and Pharaoh said no, the Nile River became red.

Interesting. In Moses we have a picture of what Jesus would be like when He came, a preview of coming attractions. Moses knew this. He said, "The LORD will raise up a prophet like me from your midst. You should listen to him" (Deuteronomy 18:15, our paraphrase).

When most people think of Moses today, they usually think about the law, since he's the one who went up Mount Sinai to meet with God and receive the Ten Commandments, along with lots of other rules for life and worship (Exodus 20–23). The apostle John referred to Moses as the lawgiver, saying, "The law was given through Moses; grace and truth came through Jesus Christ" (John 1:17). Moses was meant to lead us to Jesus, to be a placeholder until Jesus arrived.

If your marriage relationship isn't working, might it be because you're letting Moses run the show? Implementing the law's requirements of "eye for eye, tooth for tooth" (Leviticus 24:20)? Some couples live by this kind of tit-for-tat rule: *You bought this, so I can spend that. I watched the kids last week, so it's your turn. You aren't pleasing me, so I won't please you. He doesn't respect me, so I won't submit. She cut me off sexually, so I cut her off from affection.* All that leads to is a bloody mess.

If you and your spouse both allow Jesus to be in charge in your souls and in your relationship, He will lead you to a new and better way. He will not turn water to blood; He'll turn water to wine. You'll be able to enjoy and savor your marriage because of a little thing called *grace*, in which you each look at the other through the lens of the cross. When you're no longer constantly keeping score, you can freely forgive because you are forgiven.

Maybe in your relationship you need to give Moses a pink slip and let him know Jesus is taking the wheel. And if you've never given your heart to Jesus, I pray that today would be the day, that even as you finish this entry you would surrender to Him and invite Him in to be the Lord of your life. He died for you, He rose from the dead, and if you call out to Him in faith, He will save you from your sins. He will change your life from the inside out, giving you hope in death and purpose in life. So call out. Invite Him in. He's ready for you.[1]

Now, depending on what church you attend or your upbringing, you might be squirming a bit at the fact that in His first miracle Jesus made an alcoholic beverage; or maybe you're wondering why He was at a party at all when He had a world to save and people to heal and the devil to defeat. But the book of John tells us very clearly why Jesus was there: "Jesus and his disciples had also been *invited* to the wedding" (2:2).

Jesus had been invited. If you know only one thing about Jesus, know this: He will come into any situation where He is invited. Is He a part of your marriage? Did you put Him on the guest list? If you feel like He isn't involved in your relationship, it's not because He doesn't want to come—He just won't party crash. You have not because you ask not (James 4:2).

He's looking for us to invite Him into every corner of our lives—and also offer Him the ingredients for a miracle. They are always within reach. God uses what we have and, more importantly, what we give Him. We can get stuck because we focus on what we don't have, but He wants us to consider what we've been given.

So let's decide to stop keeping score and insisting on an eye for an eye. Let's take Jesus' miracles instead. Miracles require faith, and obedience is necessary for blessing. Sometimes it may seem stupid or crazy—or both—to follow God. But if the two of us have learned anything from the journey of following God, it's that if you feel crazy, you are probably doing it right.

Remember, it might not be that you have a marriage problem; it might be that you have a soul problem. Give your heart to Jesus and walk in relationship with Him. From the altar to the grave, Jesus cares about every detail of your life.

BRING IT HOME

- When do you and your spouse most often feel the need to keep score in your relationship?
- What would happen if you wiped the slate clean today?
- If Jesus shows up where He's invited, what can you do to invite Him into your relationship more often, even in the everyday details?

THE PINK SLIP

- Try keeping track of every time you want to let Moses run the show by keeping score with a tooth for a tooth. ("They do this, so I'll do that.") Jot it down.

IF YOU AND YOUR SPOUSE BOTH ALLOW JESUS TO BE IN CHARGE IN YOUR SOULS AND IN YOUR RELATIONSHIP, HE WILL LEAD YOU TO A NEW AND BETTER WAY.

HE WILL COME INTO ANY SITUATION WHERE HE'S INVITED.

- Now, turn each item on your "scorekeeping" list on its head. For every ungracious exchange that goes through your mind, hand your spouse a slip to redeem for a kind, selfless action on your part. (Or just do it without the paperwork!) It may seem crazy to fight "fairness" with selflessness and grace, but that's what Jesus does. And it just might result in miracles.

PRAYER

Jesus, we invite You into our marriage right now. You are the way, the truth, and the life, so we choose You to be the way in our relationship. Thank You for turning the law into miraculous grace. We want to do the same. Help us stop keeping score and start showing grace to each other. In Jesus' name, amen.

A man reaps what he sows. . . . Let us not become weary in doing good, for at the proper time we will reap a harvest if we do not give up.

GALATIANS 6:7, 9

CHAPTER 9

BEEF UP THAT MARRIAGE ACCOUNT

LEVI AND JENNIE

Marriages are like savings accounts: they have only what you put there through sacrifice over time, but the more you invest and the more patient you are, the more it will pay off. So how can you and your spouse end up with a big, beautiful fortune in your marriage bank—enough love to retire on and enjoy under a palm tree together somewhere? Two key things: staying the course and regular deposits.

You've probably heard about compound interest—when you leave an investment untouched to grow, your interest starts earning interest. That can give you some pretty explosive gains. For example, if you start saving one dollar a day when your child is born, by the time they are eighteen, the savings will grow to $13,000 with 7 percent interest. If you stop investing it and leave it alone, allowing it to compound, it could reach $410,000 by the time your child retires.[1] But if you keep emptying your accounts, you miss out on the benefits.

It's the same with marriage. If you abandon your marriage to start a new relationship, all you are doing is walking across the street to a different bank, opening a new account, and starting at square one with someone else; your finances stay the same. Compound interest can't take hold if you don't leave your investment in one place for an extended time.

Marriage, like a long-term investment, requires the discipline to stick it out through the ups and downs, trusting that eventually it will pay off. We can't approach marriage like a rookie stockbroker, tricked by every hiccup caused by fluctuating oil prices or orange juice shortages. We have to make a wise decision and then stick with it for the long haul.

After all the two of us have been through and fought through and prayed through together, we would never for a moment consider divorce. We have worked so hard to get where we are. We're committed to the blood, sweat, and tears we have in this investment, and we are bound and determined to watch it mature. Giving up now would be like selling Apple or Google stock to invest in a company that caught our attention on *Shark Tank*. As I (Levi) like to say, "If she ever leaves me, I'm going with her!" And I (Jennie) would really be lost without him. I've grown to depend on him in so many ways—travel, technology, reminding me of the big picture and God's perspective, and to get outside and not be a hermit. I need him!

So, continuing with the analogy of saving accounts, think about deposits. No investment in your marriage is too small to make a huge difference over time, and you can make them in all kinds of ways. In our home, Thursday night is date night. We go out to dinner and see a movie, we go on a walk, or we just stay home. We talk about deep stuff and not very deep stuff. We laugh. We cry. We ask for forgiveness and make plans. We share our dreams and fears. When we were young and poor, our date nights were trips to Costco to eat a hot dog (and samples of course). Romance can happen on any budget.

Date night is sacred and replenishing, although it has looked different in the various seasons of our lives. Our daughter Lenya went to heaven on a Thursday right after our date night, and it took a long time to go back to Thursday nights. We started doing Thursday morning bike rides, and that stuck for a while. Your dates may not look like ours, and that's okay! The point is, you're prioritizing your relationship by spending time together.

In addition to date nights, we also take little getaways together each year. It can be hard to make time for this, especially with kids, but these times have refreshed our marriage so much! It packs a bunch of fun and intimacy and rest into a few days. Side note: I (Jennie) have been discouraged at times because our day-to-day relationship often doesn't look exactly like these getaways. We come home to schedules and work and bills and busyness and our children (whom we adore, but you know how it is). I had to learn to enjoy our precious getaways fully and have the best honeymoon-like time, and then let those times fuel the rest of our regular lives. We won't always feel the highs, but we can let those times do the work of filling our tanks and accounts, as well as help us through the lows.

You will be able to enjoy the riches of your marriage to the extent that you invest in it. If you keep your accounts from running low, God will compound and multiply them. And trust us when we say this: if you don't date your mate, the devil will find someone who will. No one can stop you from having a marriage that's incredible; you just have to make regular deposits of love, generosity, forgiveness, time, affection, communication, and intimacy—and get ready, because it will grow.

BRING IT HOME

- What rough times have earned you and your spouse interest in your relationship? What did you earn from choosing to stick it out together?

YOU WILL BE ABLE TO ENJOY THE RICHES OF YOUR MARRIAGE TO THE EXTENT THAT YOU INVEST IN IT.

NO INVESTMENT IS TOO SMALL.

STAY THE COURSE AND MAKE REGULAR DEPOSITS.

YOU TAKE CARE OF THE INVESTING, AND LET GOD HANDLE THE GROWTH.

- How has your relationship "matured" over time? The past year? The past month? What can you enjoy about each other now that you didn't when you were just starting out?
- Honestly, how do your "accounts" look now in your marriage? Empty? Full? What might change if you paid as much attention to your relationship accounts as you do to your real-money accounts?

SPIN THE BOTTLE

Stumped on what to do for a fun date night? Mark six numbers in a circle and spin a bottle, or draw a number out of a hat—and whatever number you get, plan a date around that theme:

1. *Have a different food adventure.* Try a new restaurant or prepare a different kind of food at home.
2. *Do something artistic or crafty.* Go back to your elementary school days and break out the Elmer's glue, craft paper, and popsicle sticks. Maybe make it a challenge for all you competitive ones out there.
3. *Go outdoors.* Take in the fresh air together with an easy walk or something a little more active.
4. *Get cozy at home.* But plan it like a date night! Hire a babysitter if you need to, or enlist your kids to serve you a candlelit dinner. (It actually could work. We've done that twice, and the house didn't burn down.) Also, at-home dates make it more convenient for lovemaking.
5. *Wild card.* Get crazy with something you *really* wouldn't normally do. Indoor sky diving, arcade, ballroom dancing,

skeet shooting, roadside attraction, axe throwing . . .
Expand your adventure-date horizons.

6. *Mystery destination.* Just get in the car or start walking toward town with no plan, and see what happens. (We just felt the planners say, "Heck no," under their breaths, but, hey—live a little!)

PRAYER

God, You are the True Investor in people and relationships. Thank You for wanting to be with us and wanting a relationship with us. With Your heart in ours, we want to grow in how we invest in our marriage. Help us see that what we have is beautiful and strong. And help us see the potential in us as we create margin in our relationship. Change our perspectives to match Yours more and more. And help us have fun! In Jesus' name, amen.

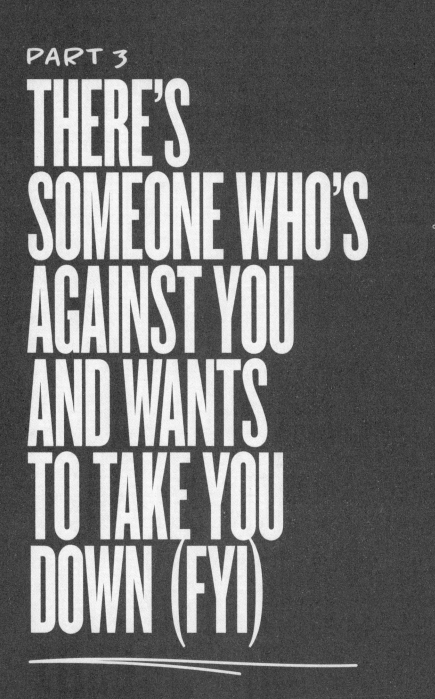

PART 3

THERE'S SOMEONE WHO'S AGAINST YOU AND WANTS TO TAKE YOU DOWN (FYI)

LOVE NOTES

[Jesus] . . . is able to do immeasurably more than all we ask or imagine, according to his power that is at work within us.

EPHESIANS 3:20

CHAPTER 10

KNOW YOUR WORTH

LEVI AND JENNIE

One of our favorite TV shows to watch as a family is *Shark Tank*. Aspiring entrepreneurs or inventors pitch their businesses or products to a group of billionaire investors to get venture capital. They explain why their new potato peeler, sponge, or grass-cutting device deserves an investment. Then, if the investors are interested in the product, they haggle over the terms.

As the investors—the "sharks"—respond to the opportunity to own a piece of an entrepreneur's company, they say what they think the company is worth and offer to trade money for a percentage of ownership. Then the entrepreneur either agrees with that value and accepts the offer or rejects it.

The sharks almost always try to undervalue the company and get it for a deal. Their goal is to own as much as they can for as little as possible. One shark, who calls himself Mr. Wonderful, is notorious for being a scoundrel. He says all kinds of loving things to his fellow sharks like, "You're dead to me" and, "You're going to get crushed like the cockroach you are." He cares only about money and is ruthlessly vocal about his desire to get more of it. He attacks the entrepreneurs and even turns on his fellow sharks.

The devil works in a similar way—with you as an individual and with your marriage. He is the worst shark of all horrible sharks. He'll always try to rip you off by offering you much less than you're worth.

It's easy to fall into the mindset that your marriage is self-sustaining or just fine the way it is and forget its true worth and the possibilities it holds. God has so much more for you and your marriage, more than you could ever think possible. But if you don't understand the worth God has given you and designed you with, then you will be tempted to settle for less. Which leads us down a slippery road.

You might feel ordinary or common, but you're not. The same goes for your marriage. Your marriage matters more than you might think. God has designed you and your marriage with a specific plan and purpose. Here is some of the vision He has for you: He intends for you to flourish and thrive.

> Your heart will rejoice
>> and you will flourish like grass;
>>> the hand of the LORD will be made known to his servants.
> (Isaiah 66:14)

He wants to give you a future full of hope.

> "I know the plans I have for you," declares the LORD, "plans to prosper you and not to harm you, plans to give you hope and a future." (Jeremiah 29:11)

He wants your marriage to be a source of joy and fun, with amazing sex.

> Let him kiss me with the kisses of his mouth—
>> for your love is more delightful than wine. (Song of
>>> Songs 1:2)

God has been seeking you. Through your life and your marriage, He wants to do "immeasurably more" than you and your spouse can "ask or imagine" (Ephesians 3:20).

God is the OG designer. He is the One who created you and your spouse. And regardless of whether you decided to invite Jesus into your marriage at the beginning of it, you are here now, and the fact that you are reading this book shows you have the desire to learn and to grow in your marriage. You can make a fresh start right now. You can allow Jesus to be the center of your marriage and invite God's creative power to be released in your relationship.

The devil loves to make you insecure about the value of your marriage and your role in it. He tries to diminish it and distract you in the hopes that you'll leave the "shark tank," having given away your entire company in a terrible deal (one that makes Mr. Wonderful rich while you work your fingers to the bone). The devil is like a shark who is always looking for prey. He knows that if you are a believer, he can't take you to hell; but if you let him, he can keep you from experiencing the joy of a healthy, thriving, Christ-centered life and marriage.

God wants you not only to know that joy but also to rise up in strength and change the world. He has in His heart a grand design for you and your spouse as individuals *and* for you as a couple. It's your calling, and you were born for it. Full disclosure, though: It's not going to happen by accident. It's going to take intentionality. When we purposefully aim to follow God's plan and not our own, our love lives are very much included and impacted.

Remember the value of your heart and life. Jump out of that shark tank and into God's plan for your life and marriage. The water is great and the possibilities are endless.

BRING IT HOME

- What do you think of the list of things that God wants for your marriage? Do you find that hard or easy to believe? Why?
- In what situations do you find yourself most easily forgetting the value of your marriage (maybe work stress, finances, health issues, etc.)? What can you do to prepare for these situations and remember God's grand design for you as a couple?
- Have you noticed the devil, like a shark, swimming around your marriage? In what ways does the Enemy and the world try to undercut the value of a God-centered marriage?

CONVERSATION STARTERS

- "My biggest hope for our marriage right now is _____."
- "What's priceless about us as a couple is _____. What's priceless about you is _____."
- "If I could take any action to protect us from the things that cause us to forget the value of our marriage, it would be _____."

PRAYER

God, we know there is a shark swimming around in these waters of marriage, and we need to be cautious and careful as we relate to and honor each other. Holy Spirit, please refresh our hearts and souls, and help us to be intentional with each other. Remind us that You not only have a plan for us, but You have a deep work You want to do in our hearts individually and together. Help us see our marriage the way You do—its value, potential, and even the beauty of the season we're in right now. In Jesus' name, amen.

LOVE NOTES

Submit yourselves, then, to God. Resist the devil, and he will flee from you.

JAMES 4:7

CHAPTER 11

TOGETHER IS BEST

JENNIE

Have you ever played the video game *Fortnite*? I haven't, but I've heard this is how it works: You get dropped into an unknown land of treachery, darkness, and incoming storms that make your world start to close in on you. As time goes on, your world gets tighter, smaller, and more closed in. You run into your opponents more, contending with them and fighting with them. Your battle is against them. The goal is to be the last person standing—the one who has killed off everybody else and is now the champion in a tiny world all alone.

The goal in marriage is *not* that. In fact, it's the exact opposite of that. The goal isn't to fight each other to the bitter end and to be the king or queen of your tiny world but to fight *through* your world together. The goal in marriage is to come through the obstacles and struggles and storms *together.*

When a marriage starts off, the future is bright. Plenty of sunshine is heading your way. A bluebird might even be perched on your shoulder. You might think, *This is the best thing ever. We get to have a sleepover every night. We can walk around in our underwear or naked, having sex in every room of the house. Life is beautiful!* And then, without much warning, it feels like the world starts slowly closing in on you. Stress creeps in. Hard things come up. Conflict happens. Your spouse turns out to have some annoying traits and habits you never saw coming, and you have no idea how to stop them from doing them.

The way you view conflict in relationships very much depends on your personality, upbringing, and family of origin. You might hate conflict. You might welcome it. Wherever you stand on the conflict-o-meter, the truth remains that it is important to the health of a marriage. This might sound weird, but it is actually necessary for growth. As you stay engaged and struggle and work through it, you can experience beautiful changes in your heart and mind and in your intimacy with your spouse.

So where do we start in getting good at conflict? We've got to be brave enough not to run from the conversation. You might be thinking, *I want to do that, but it's not what I'm used to. This is hard.* Welcome to the club! We all need to be challenged in this. I'm not an expert, but it seems to me that those of us who hate conflict just need to stay, and those of us who love conflict just need to listen. (Side note: If you're in a dangerous situation or abusive relationship, I'm not saying to stay and take it. In fact, if that's the case, you should not stay, and you should talk with a trusted counselor or friend and involve the right people.)

If you're on the same team as your spouse, you'll shift from avoiding issues to addressing them. From guardedness to transparency. From stubbornness to openness. From "me versus you" to "we'll figure this out together."

When we're on the same team, we'll come through the difficulty and challenges together. Levi and I usually say at the end of a fight, "Let's never fight again"—even though we know there's going to be another fight. We know there will be another issue. But we always want to come through shining and to stay unified.

We don't *want* to fight. We hate it. But what happens on the other side of a fight makes us stronger and causes us to cling more tightly to each other. It makes us realize that we are not against each other. We're not battling each other in a shrinking world. We have a real Enemy who wants to take us out. And the best way to do that is to divide us—to put children or in-laws between us, finances between us, schedules between us, anything you could imagine to bring disunity. The Enemy wants to take us out because he knows that *we*—Levi and Jennie together—are so much better and stronger than we are apart.

So I hope you and your spouse will hear this and believe it: *You're better together.* You're great individually, yes; but God has called you to work together to reach a world that needs to know the gospel—that Jesus loves them deeply, has a plan for their lives, and wants to use them for their good and for His glory. And the way you and your spouse handle conflict can be part of that.

Conflict doesn't have to involve a knock-down, drag'em-out fight. Conflict doesn't need to be something you avoid like the plague until it blows up. Tackling the hardest stuff together can make you stronger—when you do it with respect, kindness, and hope. Together is the best place to be. And makeup sex is actually incredible—am I right?!

BRING IT HOME

- How do you and your spouse typically approach conflict?
- When has a resolved conflict made your marriage stronger?
- How could becoming braver about conflict be a strike against the real Enemy?

THE GOAL IN MARRIAGE IS TO COME THROUGH THE OBSTACLES AND STRUGGLES AND STORMS TOGETHER.

CONVERSATION STARTERS

- "The fight I remember most clearly in our relationship is _____."
- "The best part about making up was _____."
- "I most realize that we're better together than we are apart when _____."
- "This is how my parents would fight or not fight: _____."

PRAYER

God, You have called us to bring Your love to the world. Show us where we need to grow in this area and how to best honor each other even in the midst of the most difficult situations. Give us Your perspective and Your eyes to see each other. Give us strength to be in this moment. Help us think about our future relationship and how putting in the hard work now will strengthen us then. We surrender to You to use us now, as a team, knowing that we are better together. And thank you for makeup sex. In Jesus's name, amen.

After fasting forty days and forty nights, [Jesus] was hungry. The tempter came to him and said, "If you are the Son of God, tell these stones to become bread."

MATTHEW 4:2–3

CHAPTER 12

FILL UP WITH THE GOOD STUFF

LEVI AND JENNIE

Have you ever walked into a grocery store hungry? Things just kind of jump into your cart: Hot Cheetos; Oreos; Peanut Butter M&M's; *Star Wars*–branded, baby Yoda–edition Lucky Charms; Ben & Jerry's chocolate chip cookie dough ice cream. *How'd those get in there?*

The truth is, those things wouldn't look nearly as good with a stomach full of chicken breast and broccoli. If you're getting to that inevitable point in life when your metabolism is slowing down, those treats are delicious on the lips but a disaster on the hips. Lovely on the eyes, but not so much on the thighs. Or on the energy levels. The struggle is real, you guys.

After years of coming home from the store with junk food, we've realized that we're safer at the supermarket when our stomachs are full of good things (or we just use Instacart). And it helps to keep healthy, quick options around so there's always something on hand to help ward off temptation.

In the same way, when it comes to your heart, God wants you to be a picky eater—to be careful and selective about what you bring into your heart and your life. The devil knows that hunger is the single greatest way to outmaneuver a picky eater. When you are hungry, you are much less guarded about what you eat.

That's why the devil, when he tempted Jesus in the wilderness, came when he did. The devil had no problem exploiting Jesus' hunger by talking about bread. (*Carbs*—that's more than any hungry person can bear!) Satan knew that after Jesus had fasted for forty days, even rocks would look good to Him (Matthew 4:3). The devil will wait until you're run-down to bring you temptation that promises relief. He knows just when to strike. When you are tired, when you have been fired, when you get into a fight with your spouse—that's when he'll bait the hook with comfort sin. A coworker will send you a flirty text. An old flame from high school will send you a DM. A raunchy show will appear on TV. An innocent hashtag you click will take you to a sexy photo. You'll think, *I deserve this. This will make me feel better. This will cheer me up.* It might—for a little while. But then it will make you feel worse. A lot worse.

So you have to anticipate the attack. You have to put up your guard when you are weak. When you are worn out. When you are dealing with bad news, a bad mood, or a bad day. And especially when you are hungry.

Now, we are not just talking about *food hungry.* You can also be hungry for sexual intimacy. That's why 1 Corinthians 7:5 advises wives and husbands not to cut each other off from sex except for a defined time of prayer and fasting; otherwise, long periods of sexual abstinence in your marriage beg the devil to come between you. If you are not making it your goal to meet your spouse's need for sex within the godly, healthy parameters of your relationship, you are allowing them to be hungrier than necessary. And any temptations that might come along seem more alluring.

Let's also talk about being *heart hungry.* It's easier to lower your standards when your heart has been starved. Just as you counteract food hunger with a full stomach, you can make sure you and your spouse have full hearts from spending time with God in His Word and time in prayer. So be sure to guard that time. Encourage and protect each other's need to fill your hearts. The writer of Psalm 119:11 sang about how God's Word helps us overcome temptation: "I have hidden your word in my heart that I might not sin against you." How different temptation looks when you eat the Bread of Life and drink the Living Water before going out into the world to face the day! Developing a relationship with Jesus, through God's Word, fills your heart and clears your head. Then when temptations show up, you are able to see their true price tags. You'll think, *Why would I want to give in to temptation when it would dull my love for Jesus, compromise my strength, steal from my marriage, and keep me from doing God's will?*

You won't want a mouthful of rocks—because you are already satisfied.

God gives us good things in our lives, in our faith, and in our marriages. Fill your heart by doing God's will, and you won't have room for lesser things.

CONVERSATION STARTERS

- "My go-to spiritual junk food is _____. I tend to turn to it when I'm _____ (tired, stressed, hungry, etc.)."
- "For me a healthier, better alternative to fill that craving would be _____ because my heart is really hungry for _____."
- "I love it when I see you filling up on the good stuff through _____. How can we encourage each other to fill up on what nourishes our sex life and spiritual lives?"

CLEAN UP ON AISLE FIVE

- Who says a grocery store trip can't be a date? Head out to your market together and grab some delicious, healthy snacks (maybe try something new). Or if you're strapped for time, raid your pantry and make some popcorn (we like garlic salt for seasoning, and we add Milk Duds).
- Then sit down with your snacks and share some ideas on how you can help each other by making your relationship a safe place. Be honest, laugh, and have fun.

PRAYER

God, thank You for Your kindness that leads to repentance and to real change in our lives. Give us the desire to make healthy heart, mind, and body choices. Holy Spirit, help us be more discerning in what we allow in our hearts and minds. We want to be so filled with Your Word and satisfied with You that whatever else is offered won't even look good to us. In Jesus' name, amen.

LOVE NOTES

Catch for us the foxes,
the little foxes
that ruin the vineyards,
our vineyards that are in bloom.

SONG OF SONGS 2:15

CHAPTER 13

PLANT A GARDEN

JENNIE

A couple of summers ago, I planted a tiny garden in our backyard. I couldn't believe how much work it was to create a garden in a two-by-four area. This garden produced itty-bitty strawberries, along with cilantro, parsley, and basil. It was fun, but the plants didn't come back on their own the next year. So instead of doing the hard work to cultivate our little garden again the next year, I just . . . didn't.

It takes hard work to make small amounts of progress in gardening. It's the same when it comes to marriage too. Today's verse talks about vineyards that are lush with grapes growing, perhaps ready for harvest. Think of all the effort and rain and time that went into those plants blooming and flourishing! When you've got a good and precious thing like that, it's so important to protect it.

I have a friend who planted a rose garden, and it was stunning. But she didn't get her new fence up in time, and the roses were all eaten by furry passersby—kind of like those "little foxes" in today's verse. I've read that foxes will not only eat the fruit of the vine in a vineyard; they also like to gnaw on the trunk, dig holes around it, and expose the roots.[1] They don't just eat the grapes; they destroy the entire vine.

When you first see a fox, you might think, *How could a cute little fox be a problem?* To make fox matters worse, I have a friend who lives in Washington, DC, and she sends me videos of the noises the foxes that are in her neighborhood make, and it is actually terrifying. They may seem innocent, but letting in even one can ruin an entire vineyard.

What I see from this verse is the importance of protection. We must protect the marriage relationship God has given us. How do we do this? We start by looking within and asking ourselves the hard questions: *How am I protecting my own heart? What little thing (that may seem innocent) could get into my heart and end up chewing up the roots I've worked so hard to plant? How is my personal walk with Jesus going? How am I protecting my spouse? What's it like to be married to me?*[2]

We need to be asking ourselves these questions because it's easy to look at our raggedy gardens and blame its problems on our spouses—telling them, "It's your fault." Let's instead try looking within and see if we can tell what God wants to do in our own hearts. As we've already mentioned, we can't expect our spouses to complete us. Yes, we "become one" with our spouses when we get married, but the healthy way to do that is after we're already satisfied and made whole in Jesus Christ. We can't go to our spouses expecting them to meet needs that only Jesus can; we have to look to our Savior.

If your garden of marriage isn't green and full of life, you must go back to the first things first. Cultivate your love for Jesus. Go back to the Bible, and let His Word set the pace for your life.

In Luke 10:27 Jesus said, "Love the Lord your God with all your heart and with all your soul and with all your strength and with all your mind," and then "Love your neighbor as yourself." That's super basic. Love God first. We have to get back to the basics and do first things first. The easy things to do are also the easy things *not* to do. Keep this in mind: We're not going for easy. We're going for simple—the things God asks us to remember to start with. Starting is the hardest part, but we just have to roll up our sleeves and get our hands a little dirty.

Is your marriage like a beautiful garden? Keep working at it. Don't stop doing the simple, important things to keep it growing.

Maybe the garden of your marriage isn't looking so good right now. Is it overgrown? Instead of a garden, does it look more like a battlefield with a few weeds? Then you are in the right place. The fact that you're still reading this devotional is proof that God is working in you. Don't lose heart. If you get overwhelmed and think only about what your garden is not, then you will let discouragement keep you from the strength that will keep you going and hoping and watching God move.

Are there a lot of little foxes in your garden? Start by kicking just one out. Then the next, and then the next. Don't underestimate the power of the little victories. They're huge. As you do the bits of working and tending here and there, before long, you will look up and see something resembling a garden. And your marriage will be even more beautiful because of the hard work you both did to get there. As you tend the garden of your marriage together, keep asking God for His perspective, His love, and His strength. It will change everything.

BRING IT HOME

- Where is your marriage garden thriving and flourishing? What's a specific example in everyday life?
- Where is your marriage garden dry and full of weeds? What little foxes tend to gnaw at what you're trying to accomplish?

- How can you help each other keep Jesus in the center of your lives individually? How can you keep Jesus in the center of your marriage?
- What's a way you've resolved to tend your marriage garden?
- What is your vision of a flourishing marriage?

A FOx A DAY

Let's get some of the foxes out of the garden before they destroy everything in sight. The great thing about starting small is that it gets easier and easier as we go.

Identify five little things you want to keep out of your marriage. If some things that come to mind are uncomfortable, that is totally normal. Here are a few examples:

- The fox of spiritual dryness. If you're skipping daily time with the Lord and in His Word, that will show up over time. Encourage each other in your personal time with Jesus.
- The fox of scheduling conflicts/confusion. It seems like such a simple thing, but even little bits of communication go a long way! Take a step in syncing your calendars and having a conversation or text about your schedule or things coming up.
- The fox of constant media. Consider your own consumption of media of all kinds. You might try taking a break, turning off the TV, putting your phone down and looking each other in the eyes. Maybe more hand-holding and laughing and making out.
- After you spend some time dealing with these issues, answer this: How does taking care of these little things give you hopeful momentum?

YOUR MARRIAGE WILL BE EVEN MORE BEAUTIFUL BECAUSE OF THE HARD WORK YOU BOTH DID TO GET THERE.

DON'T STOP DOING THE SIMPLE THINGS TO KEEP YOUR MARRIAGE GROWING.

PRAYER

Father in heaven, You are the Gardener of all gardeners. You not only tend to us, but You know us. You designed us for relationship with You first of all. And You knew that we would need relationship with others. In all this, You are the only One who satisfies us and fills our every need. As we seek to follow Your lead in the garden of our marriage, we look to You. Help us identify the little foxes that might even be ruining our vineyard without our realizing it. We choose to turn to You right now, and every day, so we can tend to our garden well. In Jesus' name, amen.

LOVE NOTES

The eyes of the LORD are everywhere,
keeping watch on the wicked and the good.

PROVERBS 15:3

CHAPTER 14

TO THE RIGHT, TO THE LEFT

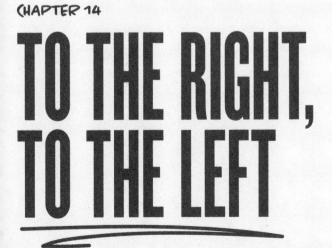

LEVI AND JENNIE

One day, Moses happened to witness an Egyptian taskmaster beating a Hebrew slave. Out of solidarity with the Hebrew, whom he knew shared his blood, he beat the Egyptian to death and hid his body in the sand. The details of the account of this crime of passion are important, and here is a glimpse into Moses' strategy: "He looked this way and that way, and when he saw no one, he killed the Egyptian and hid him in the sand" (Exodus 2:12 NKJV).

Did you catch that? This outburst of wrath (which, by the way, would cost Moses forty years of his life) came about because he looked "this way" (to the left) and "that way" (to the right), and seeing no one, he believed that the coast was clear. What he failed to do is what you and I can easily forget to do: he never looked up. Giving no thought to what heaven would think about his actions, Moses took matters into his own hands. He did the right thing (helping a fellow Israelite) in the wrong way (murdering an Egyptian taskmaster) and made a mess of things.

Let's lean in and learn from Moses' mistake. Living life looking only to the left and to the right keeps us in a selfish loop. We are only seeing life from our perspective and from others', not the perspective we're meant to keep asking for—God's.

There was a moment when Jesus' disciples asked Him how to pray. His answer:

Our Father in heaven,
hallowed be your name,

your kingdom come,

your will be done,

on earth as it is in heaven.

Give us today our daily bread.

And forgive us our debts,

as we also have forgiven our debtors.

And lead us not into temptation,

but deliver us from the evil one. (Matthew 6:9–13)

The key to living on earth is living in light of our Father in heaven. It's having the mindset that God's will would be done on earth as it is in heaven.

There is incredible power that comes from looking up and acknowledging the presence of God first—before we deal with the way we treat each other.

As you may have picked up from our opening story, I (Jennie) have dealt with moods most of my life. I have too many times to count been kind and happy with strangers, but moody and snippy with Levi. What the heck?! Something I have learned (and continue to learn) is that the more I live with my heart set on heaven, walk in step with the Holy Spirit, and cling tightly to Jesus, the more and more I live my life looking upward, in step with heaven's heartbeat, and not stuck in left-and-right living. A result? I'm kinder to those I love the most.

Our goal in life should be ending the false separation between God and us and embracing the fact that everything we say and do is being watched. Not in an oppressive Big Brother kind of way but in a loving Father kind of way. Life and relationships will take on and tap into new meaning, significance, and strength to the degree that we learn to look up at God and acknowledge His presence.

It's understandable if you are creeped out by the concept of always being watched. Whether thinking about God's omnipresence fills your heart with courage or covers you with shame has everything to do with who you think God is. If you think God is vengeful and angry, then the idea of God watching you makes you live in fear, because you imagine He is watching you like Santa Claus, and He can't wait until you blow it so He can stick coal in your stocking.

God's nature and heart aren't to catch you in the act of sin and messing up. His heart toward you is only love and grace. And His desire is for you to know that what you might choose when you only look left and right, and not up, could hurt you and hurt those you love the most.

There can be great confidence in God's surveillance. There's a Latin phrase, *coram Deo*, which means "in the presence of God." If we remember that we are living before Him, in His presence, before His face, and that He looks at us with love in His eyes, it will grow our desire to avoid doing anything that could come between us and Him. It reminds us that it's His kindness that leads us to repentance (Romans 2:4).

It's with that same kindness and love that Jennie and I want to approach our marriage. We don't want to do anything that would cause something to come between us. In Proverbs 31, one of the things that can be said of a woman of faith is that "her husband safely trusts her" (v. 11 NKJV). We want to be able to say that about both of us, because there is strength and confidence in trust. When we safely trust each other, we won't want to keep anything hidden or secret from each other or God.

Scripture invites us not to stop at merely being constantly with God, but to take the relationship to another level by experiencing and benefiting from His presence. There is nothing like the nearness of God. And for those of us who are brokenhearted or feeling crushed, He is especially close:

> When the righteous cry for help, the LORD hears
> and delivers them out of all their troubles.
> The LORD is near to the brokenhearted
> and saves the crushed in spirit. (Psalm 34:17–18 ESV)

For those of us who aren't brokenhearted but just need to be reminded of His nearness:

> The LORD is righteous in all His ways,
> Gracious in all His works.
> The LORD is near to all who call upon Him,
> To all who call upon Him in truth. (Psalm 145:17–18 NKJV)

If you have felt far from God, or have wanted to stay hidden and avoid eye contact with Him, He is right there, waiting for you to return. He's ready for you to look up, to call on His name, and to find safety and refuge and strength, both for right now and for your future.

> The name of the LORD is a strong tower;
> The righteous run to it and are safe. (Proverbs
> 18:10 NKJV)

You can find comfort in God's constant nearness and observation, and that can't help but spill over into the way you gracefully navigate nearness in marriage.

But there is hope for those of us who choose to only look left and right. While it's best to look up and consider Jesus in our decisions, there is strength and hope in remembering that while this mistake cost Moses forty years in the wilderness, God used it in his life in a powerful way. God can teach us these lessons if we choose the right way, but He can also use the mess-up to bring strength to our hearts and relationships, as well as glory to His name.

But let's choose righteousness, let's choose honor, let's choose to look up.

BRING IT HOME

- When do you feel uncomfortable about being observed by your spouse? Why?
- How can you support each other in your failures and shifty moments, so there will be no reason to hide?
- How does it feel to be constantly watched by a God who is for you?

CONVERSATION STARTERS

- "A good aspect of the fact that God is constantly watching is _____, because that means _____."
- "I'm a little freaked out that God is constantly watching because _____."

- "One way God's constant observation of me has changed me for the better is _____."

PRAYER

God, You have seen us every moment of our entire lives, and You still love us firmly. We want more of You; we want to experience Your presence in our everyday lives. Help us practice Your presence and remember that we live before Your face. Give us the strength and the perspective to cultivate this holy fear and reverence for You. We need You desperately, God. Thank You that You are near to those who call out to You. We call out to You now. In Jesus' name, amen.

PART 4

LET'S TALK ABOUT SEX AND FUN AND A SEXY, FUN MARRIAGE

LOVE NOTES

Let your fountain be blessed,
and rejoice in the wife of your youth,
a lovely deer, a graceful doe.
Let her breasts fill you at all times with delight;
be intoxicated always in her love.

PROVERBS 5:18–19 ESV

CHAPTER 15

SEX ON OUR MINDS

JENNIE

At the writing of this devotional, we are forty (it's awesome, by the way, for all you young'uns), and we have been married eighteen years. We don't know a lot of things, but we have certainly learned *a lot* over the years, and we're still learning. Our prayer for you is that you would always be in a place in your life and in your marriage where you are constantly learning and growing.

Just like any part of marriage, sex is an area where it's possible to always be growing and learning and getting better. I realize this is a sensitive topic, potentially connected to painful experiences of our own or of those around us. But, while acknowledging that sex and intimacy in marriage might need to be addressed with counseling or pastoral care, I want to talk a little about the beauty of sex within marriage.

First, a reminder: God cares about you and your marriage. He has a purpose for your marriage. He wants you to see the potential of your marriage and how He designed it to be a picture of the love of Christ to the world.

If we go back to the beginning, we remember that God's vision for marriage was that a husband and wife cling to each other, that they be fruitful and multiply, which in part means procreation, which means sex. As we've discussed before, when God designed marriage, it was for one man and one woman for one lifetime. Sex was meant to be between the same two partners for a lifetime, which means a whole lifetime of learning, growing, and figuring out how to please your spouse and to be pleased by your spouse. It requires communication, tenderness, slowing down, and being emotionally connected. It requires honoring your spouse and getting really good at giving and receiving. And while it feels really good, it's also meant to be fun!

Levi and I love today's verses because they bring us back to those first feelings of the early days. Back when we were trying not to have sex while we were dating and engaged, and then making up for lost time once we were married.

(Side note: If you had sex before marriage, please know that there is "no condemnation for those who are in Christ Jesus" [Romans 8:1]. You may have things to work through in counseling and you may have consequences to deal with, but there's no shame—only confidence and victory in Christ. Sometimes we just need to remind ourselves of whose we are, not what we've done.)

In Proverbs 5, Solomon warned his son to pay attention to his wisdom, specifically in the area of immoral women who seduce, lie, and deceive. He warned his son about where this kind of life-style would take him and about resisting instruction and correction. Then he started telling him what to do instead:

> Drink water from your own cistern,
>> flowing water from your own well.
> Should your springs be scattered abroad,
>> streams of water in the streets?
> Let them be for yourself alone,
>> and not for strangers with you.
> Let your fountain be blessed,
>> and rejoice in the wife of your youth,
>> a lovely deer, a graceful doe.

Let her breasts fill you at all times with delight;

be intoxicated always in her love. (vv. 15–19 ESV)

Solomon was bringing the focus inward. "Drink water from your own cistern." Take care of yourself, and be sure not to pour yourself out sexually to everyone. There's a purity to it. Warren Wiersbe said about this verse,

> Solomon compares married love to drinking pure water from a fresh well, but committing sexual sin is like drinking polluted water from the gutter or the sewer. Sex within marriage is a beautiful river that brings life and refreshment, but sex outside marriage is a sewer that defiles everything it touches.[1]

Solomon was saying in verse 18 that it's possible to *let* your fountain be blessed. In the dictionary to *let* means "to allow or permit."[2] And *your* means there is a possessiveness and a responsibility on your part for the relationship. If it's truly *yours*, you will care for and keep it. You have a role to play in the blessedness of your marriage. It requires work, yes, but there's also rejoicing.

Solomon continued, "Rejoice in the wife of your youth." The word *rejoice* in Hebrew means "to take pleasure in and to be glad in heart." This quite literally means with the wife you married in your youth.[3]

Everyone's story is different. People get married at various ages, and it's amazing to see God move so powerfully and uniquely in relationships. But there is something to be said about marrying young and growing old with that person. There is beauty in being older and having lived some life and then coming together with

YOU MIGHT THINK IT'S IMPOSSIBLE, BUT GOD LOVES TO WORK WITH IMPOSSIBILITIES!

IT IS POSSIBLE TO LET GOD CHANGE YOUR MIND TOWARD INTIMACY IN MARRIAGE.

your spouse, but this verse is specifically talking about being glad with and taking pleasure in the spouse of your youth.

Once when I was on a plane, I sat behind a couple—who seemed to be in their eighties—who were talking, smiling, laughing, and just being so sweet the entire flight. When we landed, I watched them get off the plane. (I sound so creepy, like I watched them the whole time, which I pretty much did.) I wondered what their story was. I could only imagine years and years of preferring each other, listening to each other, learning the hard way with each other, and working through the heartache and the pain. I also remember thinking, *I want that when I'm eighty. I want to be old and wrinkly and happy with Levi.* Even though I don't know their story, I still like thinking of them as a picture of spouses rejoicing in each other for a lifetime.

There is a sweetness and playfulness in Solomon's words in Proverbs 5. You can especially feel that the husband is meant to see his wife as delightful and graceful, precious and special. I mean, Solomon advised the husband to let his wife's breasts satisfy him at all times. (Pause for giggling or amening as needed.)

Here is the reality: Breasts are beautiful. God created women with a beauty within, but also with a captivating beauty without. Eve's figure caught Adam's attention so intensely that he wrote a poem about her. You know a guy has to be really excited about something to write a poem! But a woman's breasts are meant to satisfy her husband.

Husbands, let's be real. There are a lot of breasts out there, but I want to encourage you to be obsessed with only your wife's. Whether or not you're drawn to look at others' chests, strengthen your vision to have eyes for only your wife's breasts. And wives,

I encourage you to *let* your husband be obsessed with your breasts.

(Side note for the ladies: If you have had a mastectomy, I want you to know this verse is speaking to the overall appeal of a wife to her husband. To the way she moves and how he is enraptured by her. Please don't hide in undue shame, but trust that God has brought you two together and still intends for you to be wildly attracted to each other. Julia Child, the famous cook who pioneered TV cooking shows, had a double mastectomy, and when she was ashamed for not having breasts for her husband, Paul, he said, "I didn't marry you for your breasts, I married you for your legs."[4] Your husband loves you and the shape of you regardless of breasts or lack thereof.)

I hear of wives who don't like to be naked in front of their husbands, or they wear a bunch of clothes in bed to signal, *No sex for you!* But I like how Gary Thomas and Debra Fileta, in their book *Married Sex*, shared the story of a couple who always sleep naked, which always makes sex a possibility.[5] (I concur that sleeping naked is awesome, by the way. I'd just recommend locking the door if you have kids and keeping a robe at the foot of your bed.)

Sex is amazing for the man *and* the woman. Why do we as women tend to get stuffy and standoffish and complain that sex is always on our husbands' minds? Well, it is. But why not let it be on our minds too? Orgasms are a wonderful thing for women too—can I get an amen?! Have I said "breasts" enough times for you? Let's keep going then.

Solomon said, "Let her breasts satisfy you at all times; and always be enraptured with her love" (NKJV). At all times?! *Always* means going on without interruption, regular repetition, morning and evening; and *enraptured* carries the idea of being intoxicated and drunk on love.[6] Sound exhausting? If it does, that just means you're human. It's impossible to do everything continually, but it is possible to let God change our minds toward intimacy in marriage. And it's possible for us to grow in this area no matter where we are right now. Let that bring you hope if you need it.

(Side note for the ladies: We can struggle with hormones. At age thirty-eight, I was diagnosed with PMDD—premenstrual dysphoric disorder. This diagnosis enabled me to get the help I needed, and it has revitalized our marriage. The storms still come each month, but I'm learning how to take care of myself. All this to say, I encourage you to learn your body. If you struggle with hormones or anything else, I encourage you to get the help you need. Also, if you just had a baby or surgery or anything that will keep you from having sex for a period of time, it's okay. It's a season. Tell your husband you want him and can't wait to have sex soon; he needs to hear you say that. Also, you can get creative. Just sayin'. Hand jobs are a thing.)

My encouragement to you both is to open your eyes and your hearts to how God might be leading you to deepen this special, unique, incredible area of your relationship. You might think this is impossible, but God loves to work with impossibilities. My prayer for you two is that this would launch you into deeper communication, intimacy, and confidence as you let God lead you and build you up stronger.

BRING IT HOME

- What were your thoughts about sex growing up?
- What are your thoughts about sex now?
- Is there anything you want to talk about regarding your sex life?

GET IT ON

- Read *Married Sex* by Gary Thomas and Debra Fileta.
- Try something new in your sex life. (Examples: If you only have sex at night, try a morning delight. Or if you only have sex in bed, try the laundry room. Or try sleeping naked.)
- Make a lovemaking playlist. It definitely adds to the vibe.
- Have fun and laugh!

PRAYER

Creator God, Lord of all, thank You for the gift of sex within marriage. Thank You for creating something that feels so incredible. Thank You for the freedom and victory we have in Christ. Free us from any shame or any past hurts as we embrace and nourish this amazing part of our marriage. We choose to practice and to get better at it and to always be enraptured in each other's love. In Jesus' name, amen.

LOVE NOTES

The Lord Jesus himself said: "It is more blessed to give than to receive."

ACTS 20:35

CHAPTER 16

BUILDING A FIRE

LEVI

A while back we did a "Relationship Q&A" at our church. And a big question that people kept asking was, "How do you keep sex fun after being married for a while?"

Well, okay then. Let's get right into it, shall we?

To answer that question I would say, "Practice." The more you practice, the more fun you have. From what I've heard, it's like playing the violin. If you spend years practicing the violin, does it make you worse at it or better? Think about a Stradivarius. (It's that extremely expensive, super-valuable violin worth upward of $16 million.[1]) If you were working with an instrument of that quality, you'd want to take time to observe it, to get to know it, and to be an expert on it because it is a masterpiece.

When you think of sex with this in mind, you remember the goal of sex is to give pleasure, not to receive it. We're living in an era of increasingly automatic, VR, artificial, and (on the horizon) robotic sex, where so many people are having pornographic sex solo. But really, at the end of the day, it's so empty because it's all about taking. It's all about receiving pleasure and not about giving pleasure. The climax of sex like that leaves you with the release of oxytocin (the bonding hormone released in sex following orgasm and in breastfeeding), but with no one to bond with. That is why there is such cold despair that follows the euphoria of masturbation. The most pleasure you will ever have is in giving it and then experiencing the warm comfort of post-coital cuddling. Like Jesus said—and this is the best sex advice you'll ever get—"It is more blessed to give than to receive" (Acts 20:35).

So when your mentality is *I want to give pleasure; I want to understand my spouse in order to learn how to give them pleasure,* sex can't get old.

And you know what else? There's nothing sexier than praying with your spouse. I am serious. It's in our times of praying together—the intimacy we feel, the oneness we feel together before God, that passion—that I find Jennie most desirable. So I would say build your prayer life.

Also, try to think outside the bedroom. That's where sex begins. It's been said that sex starts in the kitchen. (And if you don't have kids, that might literally be true! Good for you guys!) The mentality of thinking outside the bedroom is starting that morning at the breakfast table and continuing with small words of kindness throughout the day.

It's that text.

That note.

That tone and sweet attitude.

When your spouse gets a text from you at two o'clock in the afternoon that says, "I'm thinking of you. I'm praying for you. I love you," it's like kindling for a fire.

When you're building a fire, you put all the wood in place, but it's the little bits—the newspaper and twigs and kindling—that make it catch fire. Those are all the things you're doing throughout the day.

It's picking up your wet towel and hanging it up. It's remembering the little things the other person loves. It's going out of your way to do something nice. It's keeping track of those things and remembering them. That's how you keep the fires of marriage blazing.

Good sex depends on how you guard yourself throughout the day too. The more you're compromising with what you're looking at, the more that erodes your satisfaction with your spouse. Ultimately, one of the big problems with pornography is that it trains you not to be pleased by the spouse God gave you. You get waylaid by the novelty and the stimulation of someone else. So it all comes down to what you don't allow and what you intentionally, consciously do. And then focusing more on giving than receiving.

So make sure you have the kindling you need to build a fire in your marriage: practice, prayer, small actions, and a well-protected mind. All these things add up to keeping things fresh and fun in the bedroom.

BRING IT HOME

- How has your understanding and knowledge of each other grown over the years as you've "practiced the violin"? How about recently?
- Have you ever thought about the connection between prayer and your sex life? How can you tie those together more?
- What do you need to guard yourselves against to protect, honor, and cherish sex within your marriage? What kinds of attitudes? What kinds of media? What else?

THE GOAL OF SEX IS TO GIVE PLEASURE, NOT TO RECEIVE IT.

THIS IS THE SECRET TO KEEPING SEX FUN EVEN AFTER YEARS OF MARRIAGE!

START IN THE KITCHEN

- Pick a day this week and start "building your fire" at breakfast.
- Prepare a special breakfast together and resolve to keep in touch throughout the day with kindnesses.
- If you know your spouse's love language, do those things.[2]
- Send loving texts (even if it's from the next room).
- Sexy texts work too.
- Remember and reflect on what your spouse loves. Give them little infusions of joy all day long.
- And at the end of the day, see how much better it is to give than to receive as you get in some good practice.

PRAYER

Lord God, it is a gift to get to know and love each other, to appreciate and be experts on each other as we enjoy the way You've made our bodies and minds. Guide us into a flourishing sex life together. In Jesus' name, amen.

Marriage should be honored by all.

HEBREWS 13:4

CHAPTER 17

BRINGING SEXY BACK

LEVI

t's amazing how messages get mixed up when communication passes through just three or four people. Think of the game of telephone, which you may have played as a kid: "I like long walks on the beach" can morph into "My cousin is choking on a peach." The farther you get from the one who spoke the original words, the more distorted the message may become.

In the same way, God's purpose and plan for relationships and romance has been obscured. We need to go back to the beginning to find out what He had in mind. One word that should mark our thoughts on sex is *honor*.

The word *honor* speaks of worth. If you honor something, you put a high value on it; you esteem it as being precious. To honor something is not to take it lightly or approach it flippantly. Scripture tells us we are supposed to show honor where honor is due (Romans 13:7). No one is higher than the Most High God, who is worthy of all praise, glory, and worship forever. This idea is all over the Bible:

> Great is the LORD and most worthy of praise;
> > his greatness no one can fathom. (Psalm 145:3)

> There is no one holy like the LORD;
> > there is no one besides you;
> > there is no Rock like our God. (1 Samuel 2:2)

> But you, LORD, are forever exalted. (Psalm 92:8)

Our honor then flows down to all people who were made in God's image. C. S. Lewis reminded us,

There are no *ordinary* people. You have never talked to a mere mortal. Nations, cultures, arts, civilisations—these are mortal, and their life is to ours as the life of a gnat. But it is immortals whom we joke with, work with, marry, snub, and exploit— immortal horrors or everlasting splendours.[1]

The honor or dishonor we show people has the potential to help them on their paths to becoming either more splendid or more horrific. When we honor people, we acknowledge that their souls are immortal and that, whether they run the drive-through at Taco Bell or crisscross the country on a private jet, they matter.

Honor should mark every relationship in our lives, especially in marriage.

Unfortunately, we live in a day when honor is in short supply. We're experiencing a drought of even basic respect. Everything about our culture is sarcastic, snarky, pessimistic, anti-authority, and rebellious, with an undercurrent of *Who are you to tell me what to do?* The millennial generation I'm a part of was raised on *Beavis and Butt-Head*, *The Simpsons*, *Salute Your Shorts*, and *The Ren & Stimpy Show*. We are a pretty skeptical bunch, as you can tell from our 280-character-long attention spans and seen-it-all attitudes. Bring this kind of mentality into the context of marriage, commitment, love, and married sex, and we have a whirlpool of confusion, misunderstanding, suspicion, indifference, and apathy.

The world could do with a great deal more honor, especially

when it comes to our love lives. The Bible tells us clearly that marriage and sex are to be honored: "Marriage should be honored by all, and the marriage bed kept pure, for God will judge the adulterer and all the sexually immoral" (Hebrews 13:4). This verse tells us we need to bring sex back to its proper place—the marriage bed. Married sex is beautiful and fun and should be honored and valued.

What does it mean to honor this gift of sex in its intended context? It starts with acknowledging that God not only designed and has a master plan for marriage but also has a specific plan for sex within marriage. Having a fire in the fireplace in your home is wonderful; it can heat up your house. That same fire, if allowed to leave the fireplace and reach the drapes and the drywall and the furniture, can burn the house down. It's not the fire that's the problem. So it is with sex—in the marriage bed, it will heat up your home, but if you let it out of that sweet spot, it can destroy your home. As we've said before, God's design for sex is one man, one woman, one lifetime (Genesis 2:4–25), yet for so many the reality is far removed from the original design. We bring the baggage of past experiences into marriage. It's going to take time and effort to work through whatever it is we've brought with us to get back to God's perfect design, but it's so, so worth it.

And that's why it's amazing that you and your spouse are reading about this together and working through these pages. Honoring God's plan for sex isn't easy, but nothing that's truly great ever is. Being broke is easy; saving your money is hard. Being out of shape takes no effort; developing a six-pack takes real work. No one likes discipline in the moment, but being undisciplined physically, entrepreneurially, financially, or spiritually can cause problems. You don't have to go down that slippery road.

MARRIED SEX IS BEAUTIFUL, AND FUN, AND SHOULD BE VALUED.

THE BIBLE TELLS US CLEARLY THAT MARRIAGE AND SEX ARE TO BE HONORED.

MARRIAGE SHOULD BE HONORED BY ALL. HEBREWS 13:4

You must be willing to fight for your marriage and for your calling. You need to fight for the sons and daughters you may have who, through the grace of God and your sweat equity, will grow up in a different home environment than you did. Fight to live a legacy that will impact and change the course of your family, your grandkids and great-grandkids. Fight for the souls of those whom God wants you to reach.

Is your marriage part of that? Will you fight together to bring honor back? Your marriage can become an incubator and starting place for honor to grow, not just for you but for the whole world.

BRING IT HOME

- Are *honor* and *sex* synonymous in your marriage? If not, why not? How could you and your spouse get to that place?
- What changes when you think of your spouse as immortal?
- How do you exalt and value each other through your sex life? Is there any way you might be undermining this or need to redirect?

CONVERSATION STARTERS

- "Here is how I see God's image in you: _____."
- "One way you have honored me that I remember and cherish is _____."
- "Some ways we can protect sex within our marriage from dishonor or disrespect might be _____."

PRAYER

Lord Jesus, we want honor and strength to be words that describe our marriage, especially when it comes to sex. Renew our attitudes and mindsets about sex, respect, and value in our marriage, and show us where we can extend honor up, down, and all around. In Your name, amen.

LOVE NOTES

[Jesus] said, "Truly, I say to you, unless you turn and become like children, you will never enter the kingdom of heaven. Whoever humbles himself like this child is the greatest in the kingdom of heaven. Whoever receives one such child in my name receives me."

MATTHEW 18:2–5 ESV

CHAPTER 18

LOOK UP, CHILD

JENNIE

A strophysicist Neil deGrasse Tyson said, "Any time I exit a building, I look up, even if there are clouds. I can tell you that kids—kids will look up when they come out, and adults just stop. We've stopped catching snowflakes in our mouth. We stopped jumping into puddles. And I, I don't want to ever lose that. In life and in the universe, it's always best to keep looking up."[1]

I love this childlike posture—this childlike vision. It's full of sweetness, faith, simplicity, and wonder. What would happen if this was how we approached our marriage relationships? I believe that is what God wants for us.

I think we can tend to overcomplicate life. Instead of curiosity, we make snap judgments. Instead of using our imaginations, we only see what there is, not what could be. God wants us to trust Him like a child does.

First, what if we embraced *a child's viewpoint* in our marriages? When you think about it, all kids have no choice but to lift up their eyes. They *have* to look up to look at their parents. I think this is one of the keys to having a childlike perspective. We're lifting our eyes in wonder and humility to our God who sees us and knows us and cares for us.

Next, what if we adopted *a child's enthusiasm*? One Bible commentator said, "The humility of a child consists of childlike trust, vulnerability, and the inability to advance his or her own cause apart from the help, direction, and resources of a parent."[2] Childlike faith asks honest questions and says what's on their hearts and minds.

This is like our son, Lennox. He is in a constant state of exuberance and enthusiasm. Everything he says almost looks like he's using his abs for it. He'll yell, "Mom! Dad! Wow!"—on tiptoe with his abs fully engaged. He shows so much intensity.

Childlike wonder and enthusiasm start to restore our relationships. And as we lift our eyes to Jesus, we start to see Him in each other. When you look for Jesus, you'll find Him—and He wants to be found by you (Matthew 7:7–8). He longs to have a relationship with you. Jeremiah 29:12–13 says, "You will call on me and come and pray to me, and I will listen to you. You will seek me and find me when you seek me *with all your heart*." Or like Lennox, with all your abs. Search for God with all your heart.

Kids are so uncynical. That's what's refreshing about them. It's easy to be a cynic. It's harder to develop an eye for Jesus, but it's vital, and especially as we cultivate our eyes for each other. When you look for Jesus in your spouse, you'll always find Him. When you run up against those difficult times in your lives, I encourage you to ask God to help you see them through His eyes. Your spouse is made in the image of God, and they are a thing of wonder.

Finally, what would it look like to have *a child's resilience*? When kids have squabbles and fights, it's amazing how quickly they make up. It's possible to choose to see conflict like they do. To not dwell on the hurt. We are meant to see each other as brothers and sisters in Christ—with a sweetness, an innocence, a joy, a love like a child. Romans 12:17–19 says, "Don't hit back; discover beauty in everyone. If you've got it in you, get along with everybody. Don't insist on getting even; that's not for you to do. 'I'll do the judging,' says God. 'I'll take care of it'" (MSG).

Look to God. Each of you have to look to Him individually. No

THERE IS A STRENGTHENING THAT HAPPENS WHEN YOU LOOK TO JESUS TOGETHER.

WHEN WE LIFT OUR EYES TO JESUS, WE START TO SEE HIM IN EACH OTHER.

WHEN YOU LOOK FOR JESUS IN YOUR SPOUSE, YOU WILL ALWAYS FIND HIM.

one can look to Him for you. But there's also a strengthening that happens when you look to Him together. So remember to look up, and watch God move.

BRING IT HOME

- What has caused childlike wonder in you recently? Like looking up at the moon or catching snowflakes, what do you want to reclaim wonder in on a daily basis?
- When you think of the way kids look up to their parents or other adults, what aspect of that do you most want to replicate in your relationship with God?
- Think back to when you were a kid. If you had known then that you'd end up with the person who is your spouse, what would have caused you delight and wonder about them?

WHEN I WAS A KID. . . .

Reclaim a little of that childlike posture with your spouse by doing something together that kids like to do. Maybe it's going for a walk and picking up cool rocks, leaves, or bugs. Or coloring. Or playing paddleball, pickleball, or a game. Or eating Popsicles. Whatever it is, keep it simple, and just enjoy each other's company for a while like a couple of kids. As you do, look for Jesus in your spouse. What do you see that brings you wonder?

PRAYER

Father God, we look to You. Restore to us simplicity, purity, sweetness, and faith. We're Your children, and we trust You. In Jesus' name, amen.

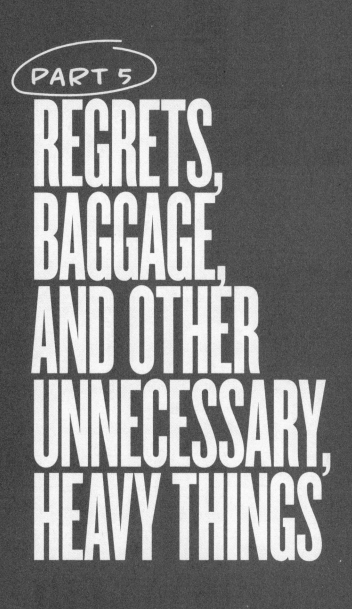

PART 5
REGRETS,
BAGGAGE,
AND OTHER
UNNECESSARY,
HEAVY THINGS

LOVE NOTES

_____

_____

_____

_____

_____

_____

_____

_____

_____

_____

_____

_____

_____

_____

_____

I am convinced that neither death nor life, neither angels nor demons, neither the present nor the future, nor any powers, neither height nor depth, nor anything else in all creation, will be able to separate us from the love of God that is in Christ Jesus our Lord.

ROMANS 8:38–39

CHAPTER 19

BAGGAGE ON BOARD

LEVI

E veryone who travels by plane brings something on board—purses, laptops, backpacks, carry-on bags. Some go in the overhead compartment; others are stowed at the feet. More checked luggage is stored in the cargo hold. Just as surely as we pack bags for trips, we all bring baggage with us into marriage.

In addition to baggage, passenger planes carry a different kind of box: a black box that records every action the pilot and copilot take. Our lives, too, are equipped with invisible black boxes. Everything we do, from birth to the grave, gets recorded, date-stamped, and logged. Altitude, elevation, transgressions, passions, sexual misdeeds—they all go in the box.

When you decided to settle down and get married, that box came with you and is sitting at the foot of your bed. Your spouse has a box of his or her own too. You can't see the boxes, because the most important parts of a person are invisible. But make no mistake: the contents of those boxes will have an undeniable presence and impact on your home. Galatians 6:5 makes it clear that "every man must 'shoulder his own pack'" (PHILLIPS).

Of the divorces you know about, is it possible that those marriages ended because of things the spouses did before they even met each other? It could be that things they hoped would stay buried—habits, debts, relationships, decisions—did not. Maybe you know about that firsthand.

One of the first things we learn after getting married is that the consequences of poor choices don't go away when you tie the knot. Everything you have done and experienced comes with you into your marriage, for better or for worse. If you're hanging your head a little right now, I'm with you. I need an emotional Smarte Carte for all the baggage I wish I hadn't packed. The good news for Jennie, and for you and for me, is that there is still hope. Even if your mistakes seem final and have hurt those closest to you, God can make a way where there seems to be no way.

Listen to me very carefully: whatever baggage you brought into your marriage is not too much for God to handle and heal. It's not too late either. You're not too far gone. Maybe it has been decades since this baggage came into your life—whether you brought it on yourself or someone else shoved it into your life— but now is the best time to give it to God and to tell your spouse if you haven't yet.

This has the potential of being a really hard moment. You're definitely taking a risk, and you don't know what your spouse will think or say or do. The most important thing is that you are listening to the Holy Spirit and letting Him lead you. As your Good Shepherd leads you in paths of righteousness (Psalm 23:3 ESV), you'll come across hard things you don't want to do. Ask God for strength; let Him lead you and fill you.

If you are the spouse being told something difficult, take a moment to pray. Ask God for an understanding heart. Ask Him to remind you of the grace you have been freely given and to give you the strength, love, and respect to freely give it to your spouse. The Bible says, "If we confess our sins, he is faithful and just and will forgive us our sins and purify us from all unrighteousness" (1 John 1:9). Just as God does for us, Jesus said, "Freely you have received; freely give" (Matthew 10:8). "Grace upon grace" (John 1:16 ESV).

YOU CAN'T CHANGE THE PAST, BUT IF YOU GIVE GOD YOUR PRESENT, HE WILL BEGIN A NEW CHAPTER IN YOUR STORY.

WHATEVER BAGGAGE YOU BROUGHT INTO YOUR MARRIAGE IS NOT TOO MUCH FOR GOD TO HANDLE AND HEAL.

AND IT'S NOT TOO LATE EITHER!

It won't necessarily be easy. There may be consequences. And you can't change the past. But if you give God your present, He will begin a new chapter in your story. Just because you can't unreap what you have already sown doesn't mean you can't start sowing something new. I dare you to believe that what feels like a big fat mess right now can bloom into a powerful message, and that someday even your sin can turn into a song—just like it did for David in Psalm 51. That's who God is and what He does. He is a redeemer of broken things. A mender of what is ripped. A healer of what is hurt.

When the Enemy wants to condemn you, his goal is to dig up your black box and rub your nose in sins that have been forgiven. But if you are under the blood of Jesus, the only way the devil can do that is by dethroning Jesus Himself—which is impossible. Psalm 29:10 says that God "sits enthroned over the flood" and "is enthroned as King forever."

No matter what you've done, if you remember to keep the blood of Jesus over you, God doesn't see your sin because you are hidden in your Savior. When you have that message locked in your heart, you are unstoppable. Nothing can separate you from the love of God. Not your baggage, not your black box, not anything. That kind of love makes us able to face anything. And seeking God's love in your marriage means you can face your baggage together.

BRING IT HOME

- What do you wish hadn't been recorded in your little black box? In your spouse's?

- In what ways would it be revolutionary to believe that the blood of Jesus covers your past?
- How would remembering God's grace and forgiveness fizzle the Enemy's condemnation on a day-to-day basis for you?

UNPACK IT

Think about this statement: "Of the divorces you know about, is it possible that those marriages ended because of things the spouses did before they met each other? It could be that things they hoped would stay buried—habits, debts, relationships, decisions— did not."

Wouldn't it be nice to unpack some of that baggage right now?

- Take a moment to pray together, asking the Holy Spirit to guide you and asking Jesus to soak your heart in His forgiveness and atonement.
- Reveal to each other one or more things you did before you met—baggage that might try to unbury itself.
- Pray for each other, bringing each thing to Jesus and declaring His power to heal.
- Resolve that these things will not bring you down: strategize ways to keep the Enemy from bringing these things back up in your marriage by continuing to turn to God.
- If you feel you've opened a can of worms that just keep coming out, visit a qualified and certified counselor to help you work through these things together and claim Jesus' victory.

PRAYER

Father, thank You for how You have brought us through what could have broken us. Thank You for how You have carried us in the midst of what we have each struggled through in our pasts individually. We choose to trust You in this moment to free us from the shame that is packed in tight with our baggage. Thank You for the way You redeem and restore and help and heal. Let Your grace cover us, propelling us into our future together. We love You. Amen.

LOVE NOTES

"I know the plans I have for you," declares the LORD, "plans to prosper you and not to harm you, plans to give you hope and a future."

JEREMIAH 29:11

CHAPTER 20

NO COMMAND-Z

LEVI AND JENNIE

Have you ever made a mistake and then felt instant regret and remorse? In today's digital world it's easier than ever to put your foot in your mouth publicly. We can now wreck our lives in a moment because nothing ever goes away on the internet. And a lot of us find out that in marriage, past mistakes can come back to bite us, no matter who was at fault. Whether they're from before you were married or more recent, how often do regrets rear their heads in your relationship? What kind of toll are they taking? What do you think could happen if you faced them head-on?

We've all done things that have made us wish we could hit Command-Z and undo the whole mess. We have a taste of how the Israelites felt when the prophet Jeremiah spoke today's verse to them. They'd been taken into captivity in Babylon because of their disobedience to God, and they were beginning to realize what had happened. Imagine their remorse as the consequences set in. They were in for seventy years away from their homeland.

I imagine they felt even worse when Jeremiah's message arrived. They were probably expecting God to say through the prophet a huge "I told you so." How shocking instead to find that the message contained an invitation to the lives they were destined to live. Essentially it said, "God's got big plans for you. There is a calling on your lives. It's not too late. You're not too far gone."

It wasn't shame but hope that marked the tone of this message. That's how our God rolls. No matter what you have done, where you have been, what mistakes you've made, or what they've cost the both of you—

whether a previous relationship is casting a shadow,

you're facing bankruptcy,

your grown children won't talk to you,

your sexual decisions have left you numb inside,

or you are addicted to a substance that consumes you—

God has plans for you. And He has plans for your marriage. Can we say that again? God has plans for *you*. And He has plans for *your* marriage.

If Scripture teaches us anything, it's that in God's hands dead things can come back to life. You can't undo your past, but there's always hope for a new beginning. The word *hopeless* isn't in God's vocabulary.

As Jeremiah put it, God wants to "give you hope and a future." Translation: He wants to move you forward to a better and brighter and stronger tomorrow.

This hope delayed speaks to the reality of consequences that remain. Forgiveness is comprehensive, but it isn't a get-out-of-jail-free card. Legal problems, loss of trust, videos preserved online for eternity—these can be the new normal that can't be ignored. This sounds discouraging, but it should encourage you. God is committed to you not for a weekend but for a lifetime. You are going to have to go through it, but you won't be alone. Even if it takes seventy years to get back home, He'll be with you every day you spend in exile.

What are you supposed to do until then? We would love to suggest this: flourish right where you are. Earlier in Jeremiah 29, God gave the Israelites marching orders for their seventy-year stint in Babylon. It's helpful to every one of us who can't get the toothpaste of our mistakes back in the tube: "Build houses and settle down; plant gardens and eat what they produce. . . . Also, seek the peace and prosperity of the city to which I have carried you into exile. Pray to the LORD for it, because if it prospers, you too will prosper" (vv. 5, 7).

How great is this? God is saying that if you can't live in the city of peace, bring peace to the city you live in. Don't endure it—enjoy it! Plant a garden. Eat some fruit. Build a house. Make the home you live in better. Give comfort to other people. Beautify your Babylon!

It's true that this advice can be super difficult to follow. But what if you focus on your walk with God and build up your heart? What if you plant some righteous seeds? How about volunteering together? Getting fit together? Going out and pursuing something good together?

Don't just mourn for what you have lost; change what you can now. God wants you to flourish right where you are! He's so good that He'll bless you in places you never should have gone.

You can't live the life you gave up, so live the life you have.

And whatever you do, don't give up! Seeds take time to grow.

BRING IT HOME

- Okay, let's go for it. What painful loss are you mourning most in your marriage right now?
- How have you worked through the grief of the consequences of your past? How have they shown themselves in your daily lives?

- How do you view the possibility of flourishing right where you are, amid the consequences? What might that look like?

CONVERSATION STARTERS

- "One way I see you living with regret is _____. But I want to help you flourish. How can I do that?"
- "This week, let's try planting a righteous seed or two and change what we can. Some little changes we could make in the midst of one of our regrettable situations are _____."
- "Is it possible that we could give comfort to others in ways we couldn't without those regrettable experiences? Those people are _____."

PRAYER

Father God, thank You for never leaving us, no matter what we've done. Please show us how to walk by faith to embrace Your beautiful plans for us, even when we can't see it or it doesn't make sense. Give us the strength to understand that we can't undo our past, but we can have hope in a new beginning. Help us learn to see how we can bring peace and comfort to our marriage, our lives, our community, and this world. We love You, Lord. In Jesus' name, amen.

Though the righteous fall seven times,
they rise again.

PROVERBS 24:16

CHAPTER 21

ROGAINE FOR YOUR SOUL

LEVI

You've probably heard about Samson's story in the book of Judges. This Israelite strongman and biblical judge fell in love with Delilah, a Philistine woman and enemy of God's people. She discovered that the power of Samson's strength was in his hair, so she tricked him into an involuntary haircut situation and chopped it off. He lost his strength, the Philistines put out his eyes, and they paraded him in chains around their temple. It was a desperate situation. Hopeless, even.

But the thing about hair is, it grows back. (Well, for most of us, anyway. Even if you're a bit hair-challenged, stay with me on this idea.)

As long as your hair follicles are living, no matter how short you cut your hair, it will keep coming back. No sooner do you shave than that stubborn stubble starts to appear.

Lean in and listen closely: no matter what you have done or how far you have run, no matter what shape your marriage is in, there is hope for you. It's possible for you to experience God's grace, forgiveness, love, power, and plan for you. The life He wants you to live is ever growing and constantly replenishing. It's not one strike and you're out, or three, or seventy times seven. God is not an angry deity with a lightning bolt, waiting to cut you down to size.

Sadly Samson never got his eyesight back. But his hair started to grow again. As his hair got longer, he became stronger—and with that newfound power came a resolve. His desire was for the enemy to pay for what was taken away. So he knocked down the pillars of the temple and was willing to take himself out to destroy God's and his enemies. God used Samson more powerfully in his weakness than He had in the rest of Samson's life. The last words out of Samson's mouth were "for my two eyes" (Judges 16:28).

Maybe you, like Samson, feel like you've lost your strength and can't get it back. Perhaps you've lost fun, romance, joy, or growth in your marriage. Maybe the consequences of a broken, chaotic world and our broken human hearts are wearing you thin. Or maybe you're terrified and feel certain that everything will fall apart in the future.

Know this: it's never too late for a fresh start. Not only can your hair grow again, but so can your soul—and with it a strengthened spirit and refreshed perspective on life.

There can be reconciliation where there was only animosity. There can be trust where there was only suspicion. I have seen marriages that were seemingly over—and then, all of a sudden, they weren't. Never forget we serve a God whose Son was dead—until He wasn't. God can and wants to make a way where there is no way. I'm not saying it will be instant, clean, or easy; but if you give God the space, He will bring new stubble from the rubble. He will help you slowly but surely build bridges of trust where there have been severe heartache and severed relationships.

Plus, God has a unique way of using these situations to be monumentally helpful to other people.

There is a couple in our church who springs to action when they learn of a marriage on the rocks, especially if there has been infidelity. Like frontline workers in an intensive care unit, they do everything they can to nurse the relationship back to health. We have seen God use their ministry in mighty ways.

But years ago it seemed their own marriage was not going to make it. I remember the tears, the anger, and the sadness they were experiencing when God put it on my heart to tell them that, as impossible as it seemed, they were going to make it. Furthermore, I added, I believed a day would come when we would send couples to them to be ministered to in the very area that seemed to be killing them. Their eyes betrayed their incredulousness and doubt, but here we stand today—they are mighty and strong, and they've made the devil pay for their two eyes.

Today's verse says that even if a person "falls seven times," he can "rise again." In the Bible the number seven stands for completeness.[1] The verse isn't saying that after the eighth fall, it's over; it's saying that no matter how devastated your life seems, you can still get back up.

Get back up.

The end can be better than the beginning.

Remember, what's powerful about Samson's story is that his eyes never grew back, but his hair did. Even if God doesn't heal or deliver the same way you ask, and even if some consequences linger, He can work in the midst of the dysfunction to bring good things, and most importantly, to bring glory to His name. If that is the case—even if things start falling apart—make your desire mirror Samson's: to make the devil pay for what he has taken away. How? Whenever you are at your darkest, shine your brightest.

BRING IT HOME

- Where would you start to "make the devil pay for what he has taken away"? In what ways can you two shine brighter for having struggled?

IT MAY NOT BE INSTANT,
CLEAN, OR EASY

GOD CAN WORK IN THE MIDST OF THE DYSFUNCTION TO BRING GOOD THINGS.

AND MOST IMPORTANTLY,
TO BRING GLORY TO HIS NAME!

- Where might you have lost hope in your marriage? What does it mean that Jesus can replenish it and cause stubble to grow from the rubble?
- Where has trust possibly dwindled in your marriage? What might happen if you offered it to God for healing?

GET BACK UP

- Share with your spouse some ways you've fallen, where you've gotten back up or will vow to get back up. These can be individually or in your marriage.
- What does getting back up look like in these instances? How can you lean on God's strength and power to invite something good to grow there?

PRAYER

Lord God, You make endings better than beginnings. But even more than that, You are somehow able to use the messy middle and the process to beautify and strengthen us. Wow. We are humbled and floored by Your love and Your kindness to us, even when we have made the mess and put ourselves in the situation. Thank You that You make a way where there is no way. Thank You for shining through us and for giving us the courage to get back up. In Jesus' name, amen.

Honor your father and your mother,
so that you may live long in the land.

EXODUS 20:12

CHAPTER 22

STAY HUMBLE AND SHOW HONOR

JENNIE

How did you first learn about what marriage is? Many of us got it from our parents or grandparents. That example may have been happy and warm, or it may have been broken and dysfunctional. Or anywhere in between. Or not there at all. No matter what our family of origin was like, when we were children, we stored away ideas of what a marriage should or shouldn't be based on the generation before us.

What are we supposed to do with that? Clearly it's going to affect us and our relationships. So how do we approach these issues of where our marriage ideas came from as we navigate our own marriages?

Well, I believe it's going to take humility and honor to dig through this together. Humility and honor toward the elder generation, as opposed to the pride that can so easily well up in us and the disrespect that can sneak in, especially when we don't understand someone else's life. It's reasonable that younger people find it hard to understand the ones who came before them because they lived in a different age with different expectations, ways of dressing and communicating, thoughts of the male and female role. And certainly with different views of life and marriage.

Honestly, I sometimes feel like I was born in the wrong decade. I have a hard time keeping up with Levi and his technological knowledge, but I get along well with elderly people. I could hang out with my senior citizen friends all day and ask them questions and learn. It just feels natural. But I get how it's hard to understand people who aren't in the same season of life as we are. And it's easy to judge. It's easy for older people to think, *Well, I know better than you because I've lived longer,* or for younger people to think, *I know better than you because you don't even email.*

Even in the midst of the generation gap, there should be a willingness to understand and humility to ask what really went on in those past situations that affected our views of marriage. And for some of us, this will translate into seeking counseling from a qualified professional to discuss ways to move forward through trauma and things we wish hadn't happened around us or to us.

It takes humility. C. S. Lewis wrote disparagingly of "chronological snobbery," which is basically when you read about someone who lived hundreds of years ago and you automatically judge them. You think you would do so much better than they did in the age they were in.[1] You don't give them the benefit of the doubt—that they were doing the best that they could in the age that they were living in with the resources they had. They only knew what they knew. They didn't know what they didn't know. Lewis was not making excuses or justifying any of the many horrific things that happened in the past. But he was saying that the easiest thing in the world to do is to assume that you somehow know better than those who came before you.

And the truth is, it's easy to practice historical intellectual snobbery when we're talking about our parents' and grandparents' generations—about the things they did or didn't do in their marriages and relationships, and the examples they gave us. We might assume that our grandparents are clueless and that our parents don't know anything because they don't have the cultural awareness we have baked into us.

But we can't write them off. When we decline to stand on the

WE CAN POSTURE OURSELVES IN HUMILITY AND GROW IN COMPASSION.

IT IS IMPORTANT TO LIVE WITH HUMILITY AND HONOR TOWARD THOSE WHO CAME BEFORE US.

shoulders of those who have come before us, and we assume they know nothing or can offer us nothing, we miss out. And we certainly lack the humility and honor God calls for.

In the family of God there's meant to be a whole stack of people standing on one another's shoulders, learning from mistakes, helping one another up. (And in the family of God we have many of those who are older to look to and honor in addition to those who raised us—amazing!)

It is so important to live with humility and honor toward those who came before us. And, by the way, this also means that we need to take care of our aging parents. If this hasn't come up in your marriage yet, it will. The Bible says to honor your father and mother (Exodus 20:12). When you're young, that looks like obedience and respect, but when your parents begin to age and health declines, it looks like taking care of them. However that shakes out for the two of you as husband and wife, it will be wise to consider what this might look like for you.

Regardless of the examples of marriages that we learned from and that painted the picture of what marriage is for us, it's possible to posture ourselves in humility, to grow in empathy and compassion for our parents, and to remember that God gives grace to the humble (James 4:6). He gives more grace, and I believe God has greater depths and grace and joy as you both continue to give these things to the Lord, and let Him grow you in honor and humility.

BRING IT HOME

- How do you think your parents' relationship affected your view of marriage? In what positive ways? In what negative ways?

- What is one thing you'd want to repeat in your marriage that you learned from older generations? And one thing you definitely want to avoid?
- Is honoring your parents/elders built into the structure of your marriage? How can you infuse more humility and honor into those relationships?

CONVERSATION STARTERS

- "I tend to dismiss my parents/elders in matters of _____."
- "When I think about building on the shoulders of those who came before us, I'm grateful for the way they _____, so we can have a leg up."
- "When I think about the challenges that came from both of our upbringings in the way we view marriage, I'm so glad we're aware of _____, so we can do things like _____ to overcome."

PRAYER

Lord God, You appointed the time that You brought us into the world, and you set us in our families. Give us the strength and grit to continue forward, building on what has come before us with honor and humility. Heal us, and show us how to love, honor, forgive, and grow as we live this life You have given us. In Jesus' name, amen.

PART 6

PRIDE SEPARATES US FROM GOD, AND HUMILITY DRAWS US CLOSER TO HIM

LOVE NOTES

Pride leads to destruction;
humility leads to honor.

PROVERBS 18:12 CEV

CHAPTER 23

HONOR
ROLL

JENNIE

When I was in high school, I was on the honor roll. Basically, if you had a certain grade point average, your name would be included in a list of students who maybe worked a little too hard on academics. I don't know if it helped people get into college, because I never went, so it'll be a mystery for the rest of my life. But yes, I (Jennie) was on the honor roll. And as if the honor roll wasn't enough, I was also the recipient of something called the President's Award when I was a senior. Sounds pretty fancy, huh? To be honest, I don't even know what it was for. I didn't have the highest grades, and I wasn't involved in a lot of things. Maybe it was just because I was a pleasant high schooler. Who knows?

As I was thinking about being on the honor roll and this award, I imagined how silly it would be if I took my award with me wherever I went. What if I brought my award into every job interview? What if I brought it into every relationship? I could use that to say, "See? Here's proof that I am a nice person and that I can do good things and that I am honorable. Case closed."

That wouldn't get me anywhere. I would like to think that I am still nice and in the president's circle of honor in life. Getting those awards in high school was great for that time. But I still have to show up each day with a heart of honor and humility *now*.

Honor isn't something you do once, get a gold star, and it covers you for life. It's an everyday action. Just like saying "I do" on your wedding day doesn't automatically mean you will naturally and easily keep your vows and love and honor and respect your spouse. You have to show up and decide to commit—to practice kindness and love your spouse—every day. Humility and honor have to happen initially and then keep on happening. And honor won't happen by itself. It takes practice and more practice, doing it when you feel like it and especially when you don't.

Honestly, God has taken a tiny screwdriver into my heart to tinker with this very thing. Lately I've been trying to analyze when I get moody or frustrated or angry. And I've noticed that when I'm doing well, when my relationships are fulfilling, fun, and happy, there is underlying humility on my part. But when things are not going well, and when I am easily angered, frustrated, overwhelmed, and snippy, humility is not there but pride definitely is.

Pride is what we're going to talk about today, because pride can knock you straight off the honor roll.

What is pride? Pride focuses on self.

Proverbs tells us that pride leads to shame (11:2 NKJV). Pride leads to conflict. "Pride goes before destruction, a haughty spirit before a fall" (Proverbs 16:18). It ends in humiliation. Pride is arrogance, cynical insensitivity to the needs of others. It's presumption.

This sounds so ugly. And that's why it's so hard to admit to. And it's important that we do before it becomes a problem.

Pride is both an attitude and an action that makes oneself out to be better than others. A prideful person shifts ultimate confidence from God to self. In Proverbs 6, we see a list of things that God hates (vv. 16–19). And at the very top of the list is "a proud look" (NKJV). Even a rolling of the eyes—God hates that.

Oh man. I don't know how that hits you, but it's super convicting to me. Because even though it's been a few decades since I've been in high school, I've definitely had major eye-rolling moments with my husband. I am not proud of those times that I chose to respond to him with a proud and selfish look.

I think God hates this proud look because He knows what it does to us. He knows that pride keeps us from intimacy with Him and from intimacy with our spouses. Pride destroys intimacy— and not just the romantic kind within marriage but intimacy in any relationship where the goal is familiarity, friendship, or closeness.

A prideful person takes honor for him or herself. But humility enables God to honor that person whenever He wants.

We see this picture in Luke 18:9–14, where Jesus told this parable:

> Two men went up to the temple to pray, one a Pharisee and the other a tax collector. The Pharisee stood by himself and prayed: "God, I thank you that I am not like other people—robbers, evil-doers, adulterers—or even like this tax collector. I fast twice a week and give a tenth of all I get."

Oh, you have the President's Award—congratulations, sir.

> But the tax collector stood at a distance. He would not even look up to heaven, but beat his breast and said, "God have mercy on me, a sinner." I tell you that this man, rather than the other, went home justified before God. For all those who exalt themselves will be humbled, and those who humble themselves will be exalted.

What's the point? When you take the role of honor and humility, God puts you on *His* honor roll. And that's the only one that counts.

BRING IT HOME

- What would happen if you tried to analyze when you are moody or angry versus times when you are in a good mood? How do humility and pride tie in to those situations?
- In your life and in your past, how have you seen pride destroy intimacy? How have you seen humility build intimacy?
- How does God treat those who admit they are sinners and ask for mercy? How can He work with them, as opposed to a prideful person?

CONVERSATION STARTERS

- "When have you felt honored by me?"
- "When have you felt dishonored by me?"
- "What are three humble things I could do to get on your honor roll? What can we do together to get on God's honor roll?"

PRAYER

Our Lord and our King, we desperately want to choose honor—to honor You above all and to honor each other no matter what. Give us the eyes to see and strength to continue to choose honor when it's easy and especially when it's hard. When pride shows its head in our hearts, help us to choose humility, to let go, and to return again to You and to each other. In Jesus' name, amen.

LOVE NOTES

Too much pride brings disgrace;
humility leads to honor.

PROVERBS 29:23 CEV

CHAPTER 24

HOW TO SPELL
HUMILITY,
PART 1

JENNIE

This week we are looking at a tool that will hopefully help our relationships: the tool of *humility*. This is a key ingredient of a healthy marriage. Really, it's important to enter *any* relationship, any situation, any interaction, with humility. It brings strength and honor to any place you use it. If you're looking for a way to build strength and honor in your marriage, humility will take you there.

Today's verse tells us that pride lands you flat on your face, but humility prepares you for honor. Pride is the slick patch under your feet, and it will take you down in a heap. Committing to humility is like moving to solid ground, or at least spreading some sawdust on that slippery spot so you can move forward together.

What it comes down to is pride destroys intimacy, but humility unlocks rich relationship.

I love acrostics, so go with me on this word adventure. We're going to walk through the word *humility* together during the next few devotions in a way that hopefully will help you remember it. I'm going to spell it out for you. Let's start with the first letter.

H is for *health*.

When you have a *healthy* spirit, you're going to be humble. When your body is healthy, it's easier to focus on the health of your whole body. When your mind is healthy, your brain and body can function as they were designed to. But if a part of you is sick, you're focusing on that one part of your body. And that part of your body draws all the attention to itself. This is not healthy; something needs attention to get things back in balance.

Your relationships can't be healthier than you are. Maybe you're trying to have a healthy relationship, but you can't do that if you're not healthy yourself. So give your heart, soul, mind, and body some attention.

As it is well in your soul, you'll be able to truly approach your relationships with a sweetness and humility that wouldn't be there on its own. Humility comes from a *healthy* spirit.

U is for *understanding*.

Understanding is making the effort to empathize and see where the other person is coming from. I know for me, in moments when I'm in a heated argument with Levi—or let's just call it what it is: a fight—I don't automatically think, *Okay, self, let's think clearly here. Where's Levi coming from? What's he gone through today? How's he doing? Why do you think he said this?*

I'm really only thinking about how what he did affected me and how what he said hurt me. Developing *understanding* turns that around, because instead I'm choosing to think, *I want to understand. I want to hear what he's saying, and I want to have a heart of understanding.* Empathy helps with this.

Truthfully, this takes practice. My heart fills with sadness when I think about the times I have learned the hard way—when I have hurt Levi in my response to him because I did not try to understand him, and I spoke rude and disrespectful words I can never take back.

But that's when I have to remember that we get to practice kindness. We get to practice understanding. We won't always get it right, and we'll mess up and speak out of line, and just be plain mean sometimes, but we can get back up and keep showing up. A counselor once told me that when I speak in a rude way, or I'm

PRIDE DESTROYS INTIMACY, BUT HUMILITY UNLOCKS RICH RELATIONSHIP.

THIS IS A KEY INGREDIENT OF A HEALTHY MARRIAGE.

not in control of my spirit, it's a healthy thing to say, "I'm sorry, I didn't say that the right way. Can I get a do-over on that?"

Don't get discouraged when you don't get it right. In humility, keep choosing an understanding heart, and keep practicing. You will get stronger, and it will get easier to choose the right way; I have experienced this firsthand.

It also helps to put yourself in your spouse's place or in their shoes. To think, *What was it like to come home to this chaos? What was it like to come into my office and feel this way?* Seek to understand the love of your life and understand where they're coming from. It really brings stability to a slippery situation.

M is for *meekness*.

The words *humility* and *meekness* are often used together in the Bible—they're interchangeable. But meekness is strength under control. It's not thinking less of yourself, but it's thinking of yourself less. For me, growing up in the church, I would hear this word, *meek*, and think of a joke someone told me once that "Meek is like me—ick." Basically, to view yourself as low and insignificant. So in my young brain, I thought that meekness meant, "Oh, I'm the worst. And I don't really know what I'm doing." But that's not what it is at all. Meekness is a strength and a power, but it's under control. It's choosing to think of others, and knowing that God has given us the strength and grace to do it.

I love how Matthew 5:5–6 says, "Blessed are those who are humble," or meek. "They will be given the earth. Blessed are those who are hungry and thirsty for what is right. They will be filled" (NIrV). I just love the way that is put. "Blessed are those who are free of pride." That's what meekness is—when you're free to be yourself, who God made you to be. And you're free to love the people in your life, to encourage and build them up, using all that extra energy you have since you're not fighting for your pride all the time. It's so good. *Meekness* is a word we need to take back.

So these are the first three letters, putting the *hum* in *humility*: *health*, *understanding*, and *meekness*. This is a good start to building solid ground together. Take some time to talk about this, and we will keep going with this next time.

BRING IT HOME

- What does humility look like in your life currently? What about your spouse's life?
- How is a healthy soul the same as a humble soul?
- How could you reclaim meekness as strength under control? What would that look like for you?

CONVERSATION STARTERS

- "A specific time you've impressed me with your humility is _____. That made me feel _____."
- "A specific time that understanding, someone putting themselves in my shoes, has made a big difference to me is _____. It mattered because _____."
- "When you and I are having a disagreement, how can we signal each other to try understanding and seeing things from the other's point of view? How can we change course in those tense times?"

PRAYER

Lord God, please show us how to grow in our health, understanding, and meekness. We want to make humility a hallmark of our marriage. In Your Son's name, amen.

LOVE NOTES

Trust God from the bottom of your heart;

don't try to figure out everything on your own.

Listen for God's voice in everything you do, everywhere you go;

he's the one who will keep you on track.

Don't assume that you know it all.

Run to God! Run from evil!

Your body will glow with health,

your very bones will vibrate with life!

PROVERBS 3:5–8 MSG

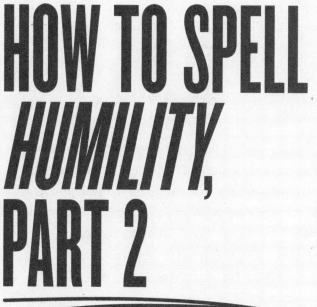

CHAPTER 25

HOW TO SPELL *HUMILITY,* PART 2

JENNIE

I n our last time together, we started spelling through the word *humility* because (a) acrostics are fun, (b) I am a spelling bee queen (Sorry, not very humble, but it's true!), and (c) humility is one of the most important stabilizing forces in a marriage. It's completely, utterly indispensable. So whatever we have to do to help you leverage the tool of humility in your marriage, it's worth doing.

We've already talked about *health*, *understanding*, and *meekness*. All these things cover up the slippery surface of pride with some gripping power. They help you gain traction and move past blame, pride, and cycles of making each other mad and frustrated. If that's not an amazing tool, I don't know what is.

So in our acrostic,

H is for *health*.
U is for *understanding*.
M is for *meekness*.
Now let's break down the next few letters.
I is for *intention*.

We must be intentional with how we approach our interactions with each other. When we're intentionally humble, it steers us in the right direction. It's like keeping your hands on the wheel as you drive a car. If you take your hands off, you're going to drift. And you never drift in the right direction. So my goal is to be humble—to have a loving relationship full of respect for my husband, to be kind and tender with my kids, and to be compassionate with the people in my life—and if I let go of the wheel of humility, it's not going to automatically go where I want it to go.

Some cars have an indicator on the driver's seat that buzzes when the driver drifts off course. It's a little poke in the rear: *Get back on the road! Watch out for that car!* I wish we had that to keep us intentional in relationships, to keep our hands on the steering wheel of humility. We absolutely must course-correct when we feel pride drifting in. And that's where the Holy Spirit comes in. As we surrender to His leading, and ask to hear His voice, He will speak and nudge and lead.

The times that get me the most offtrack with Levi come when I let myself drift. I'm no longer being intentional to walk in humility because I'm letting myself focus on the wrong things. And believe me, I can start focusing on the wrong things *fast*. It usually starts with my being hungry, and then hangry, because I tend to forget to eat during the day. All of a sudden, it's 3:00 p.m., my tummy is empty, and whoever walks in the front door first will get an angry mama. And I don't even have to tell you that when mama ain't happy, nobody wants to be home. But *hungry*? That goes back to the health part of humility too. Don't forget to eat, people.

It's also hard for me to be intentional when I let little issues cloud my whole view. Levi and I have talked about it many times, how when storm clouds roll in for me, it's really hard to shoo them away. One little negative thought can cloud my perspective on big things. I have to be intentional with fighting for the right perspective. I have learned recently the power of a good emotional toolbox. Things like: (1) breathe; (2) think about things that help you calm down; (3) exercise (like literally go to the other room and do twenty-five jumping jacks); (4) count to ten; (5) pray something like, "God, please fill me up with what I need and what only You can give me right now."

The Word has this to say about intentionality: "Be very careful, then, how you live—not as unwise but as wise, making the most of every opportunity, because the days are evil. Therefore do not be foolish, but understand what the Lord's will is" (Ephesians 5:15–17). You could say intentionality is "making the most of every opportunity" instead of letting things land where they may. Intentionality keeps us from landing in a mess, and it takes awareness and mindfulness and the heart to work.

Back to our acrostic. In *humility*, *L* is for *listening*.

The most important listening we do is to God. That's why I love today's verses so much. Verse 6 tells us that listening is huge in humility. It says, "Listen for God's voice. . . . Don't assume that you know it all," which is basically a prescription against pride.

This flows to how we listen to people too. We have to listen more than we speak and ask questions, because we don't know it all! I feel like God has been teaching me lately to ask better questions. That doesn't come naturally to me, so it's something I have to work at. Deep questions don't exactly flood my mind when I'm listening to Levi, but since he loves to process verbally, he appreciates it when I try. Instead of saying, "I don't know," I try to meet him where he's coming from as he brainstorms out loud. It's not my wheelhouse, but making the effort makes a difference.

I don't know about you, but as I'm getting older, listening has become more difficult. Whether it's listening to Levi telling me something, or our children, or anyone, I feel like I have to focus hard not just to listen to the words but to be in the moment and listen to what they are saying and how. And it's not even because of my phone or computer or things I'm doing; it's my own mind's inability to focus.

I recently found out I have inattentive ADHD, so I may need to work a little harder, but I want to be in the moment with whoever is in front of me. When Levi is telling me something, I want to be receiving and hearing and ready to exchange thoughts. I don't want to just hear; I want to be engaged. So I'm finding these days that asking is better than speaking, and so is *actually listening* to the answers. Actively listening with humility is listening in an engaged way. Add that to intention, and you are well on your way to reaping the benefits of humility in your marriage.

BRING IT HOME

- When do you find yourselves veering off the road of humility? What is usually the cause? What makes you pull toward pride? Busyness? Tiredness? Something else?
- If humility doesn't come accidentally but intentionally, what actions can you take to keep your hands on the humility wheel?
- When we know each other well, it's easy to think we know it all. What can you do to start listening to each other's hearts instead of assuming?

THE ASK-ME GAME

Set aside some time, at a meal or just sitting cozily on the couch, to ask each other some intentional questions.

- Beforehand, separately assemble twenty "deep" questions

IT'S "MAKING THE MOST OF EVERY OPPORTUNITY" INSTEAD OF "LETTING THINGS LAND WHERE THEY MAY."

WE MUST BE INTENTIONAL WITH HOW WE APPROACH OUR INTERACTIONS WITH EACH OTHER.

each. (You can use Google for this—try things like the *New York Times'* "36 Questions That Lead to Love"[1] or BetterHelp's "25 Questions to Get to Know Someone Deeply,"[2] and jot down any questions you don't really know the answers to for your spouse.) Make sure your questions are open-ended and not yes-or-no, and avoid questions that could cause a conflict.

- Take turns asking questions, and for each answer, ask two follow-up questions about what your spouse said. It may help to repeat back to them what they've shared in the process. Don't weigh in with your opinion unless they ask you to.

- As you wrap up or have dessert, do a postmortem. What was hard about listening and asking questions? What worked? What didn't? What did you like? What felt odd?

PRAYER

God, please give us the strength and focus it will take to make the decision for humility, and make us as attentive and curious as when we were first getting to know each other. In Jesus' name, amen.

LOVE NOTES

[Jesus] got up from the table, took off his robe, wrapped a towel around his waist, and poured water into a basin. Then he began to wash the disciples' feet, drying them with the towel he had around him.

JOHN 13:4–5 NLT

CHAPTER 26

HOW TO SPELL *HUMILITY,* PART 3

JENNIE

We've been learning a new way to spell *humility*. It's not just keeping your head down and biting your tongue. It's so much deeper and stronger than that. And it is key to stabilizing your marriage.

So let's review:

H is for *health*.
U is for *understanding*.
M is for *meekness*.
I is for *intention*.
L is for *listening*.
That brings us to the second *I*.
I (number two) is for *insight*.

It was a tough choice between *insight* and *intimacy* for this one, but you could say one leads to the other, so it's kind of a two-for-one. Offering insight, basically, is humbly helping others understand us better. It's like a counterpart to listening. Sometimes I assume Levi knows what I'm thinking. *He knows how I feel about that.* But nope. Even as close as we are, he can't read my mind. And your spouse can't read yours either.

So when we offer insight, we are opening up and offering an explanation. We're saying, "Well, this was how I felt when . . ." In a kind, humble way, it's explaining who you are on the inside. That's part of vulnerability and intimacy; it's letting your guard down and explaining who you are, the dreams that you have, the struggles you have, how an interaction made you feel. In a marriage that means we offer insight to each other and accept insight from each other in a loving way. It's letting our spouse have sight inside our souls, being vulnerable and willing to let them in.

Proverbs 8:14 says, "I have counsel and sound wisdom; I have insight; I have strength" (ESV). All these things come together. Wisdom, strength, and insight are a winning combo for your marriage.

The next letter, *T*, is a bit special. (Well, they're all special, but this is special to me.) It'll take some explaining.

T is for *take a towel.*

Being humble means taking the position of a servant, a giver, like Jesus did in today's verses. This picture of our Lord and our Savior getting down on His knees, taking a towel, and washing His disciples' feet is so stunning. This is something we can do every day in our marriages as we serve each other without expecting anything in return. Our Savior took a towel. In humility we can be willing to get down on our knees and to take a towel—to serve and to give.

It may not be reciprocated in the moment. But a servant's heart gives no matter what. And so my encouragement to you is to give and serve no matter what is given back. Mark 10:45 says, "That is what the Son of Man has done: He came to serve, not to be served—and then to give away his life in exchange for many who are held hostage" (MSG).

Y is for *yield.*

Think about a four-way stop. You don't just plow through one of those intersections. You have to hit the brakes and yield. You have to look around and see, *Okay, there are three other cars. Who got there first?* Then maybe, if you're like me, you think, *I'll just hold back and let everyone else go ahead because I don't want to deal with figuring it out.*

In a marriage, though, it's important to yield—to assess the situation. First, we yield to the Holy Spirit, being sensitive to what He might be speaking to us in the moment. If you yield to the Spirit in your conversations and look for how He might be leading you, you might be able to encourage your spouse in a way that you would have missed if you'd rushed in.

Then there's yielding to others, where you're not just doing what you feel, or just rushing in and doing what you think needs to be said, but waiting to see what's really going on with them. Hebrews 12:14 says, "Strive for peace with everyone, and for the holiness without which no one will see the Lord" (ESV). It's better to yield and humble yourself than to rush in and be humbled. Better to slow down on your own than to crash out of control.

So there's a new way for you to spell *humility.* As you strive to walk in humility, remember we're covered in His grace. James 4:6 says, "God opposes the proud but gives grace to the humble" (ESV). God gives you grace as you bring humility into the center of your marriage. And His grace heals. As you take steps in this direction, you'll see.

BRING IT HOME

- When have you assumed your spouse could read your mind, and you were surprised when they didn't? What insight could you have given your spouse so they could really understand?
- What can you do to make your marriage a safer space for

WISDOM, STRENGTH, AND INSIGHT ARE A WINNING COMBO FOR YOUR MARRIAGE.

INSIGHT MEANS HUMBLY HELPING OTHERS UNDERSTAND US BETTER.

opening up with insight when you feel misunderstood? What keeps you from doing this?

- Where do you tend to barrel ahead instead of yielding and slowly considering each other? What Slippery When Wet spots do you tend to crash at?

TAKE A TOWEL

This week, separately, write down one way to serve each other with humility every day, and do that thing. You can, of course, literally give your spouse a foot bath or a massage, or take something off their plate that you know they don't like. But the important thing is to do acts of service with a humble heart, not expecting anything in return. At the end of each day, guess what the other person's act was. How does this change the tone in your household?

PRAYER

Holy Spirit, help us yield to You and to each other. As we serve and open up to each other, bring to our minds the ways we can make our marriage safer. Show us how to be like Jesus in our humility—to take a towel and serve. In Jesus' name, amen.

PART 7

THERE'S ALWAYS ROOM TO GROW IN COMMUNICATION

LOVE NOTES

God is not a God of confusion but of peace.

1 CORINTHIANS 14:33 ESV

CHAPTER 27

LEVEL UP

LEVI

Communication. It is the lifeblood of marriage. We're always growing in this, always working on it, and always trying to improve it. It's vital to communicate well.

We've talked about conflict in marriage, and that goes hand in hand with communication. Whenever you have conflict, you have issues you need to talk through, but you can trust that on the other side of it will be a stronger marriage.

It's kind of like the old-school video game Super Mario Bros. When you finish a level, you go up against whatever bad guy is waiting for you. You fight that big enemy. But after you defeat that enemy, you finally get to go to the next level, and if you do this long enough, you eventually get to Bowser—the biggest, baddest of them all. We've found that it can be similar in marriage—new levels, new devils. When we fight, we can feel like we're battling each other. But it changes everything when we try to remember that when we're fighting, we're not against each other; we're on the same team. And if we can make it through that fight, and learn and grow from it, we can make it to the next level in our relationship.

The battle isn't against flesh and blood, "but against the rulers, against the authorities, against the powers of this dark world and against the spiritual forces of evil in the heavenly realms" (Ephesians 6:12). It's intense, I know, but true.

And when we remember that we as spouses aren't fighting against each other, then we can help each other fight fair and give each other insight into our minds.

When you're frustrated, it can be good to ask yourself, *Does my spouse know how I feel right now? Am I expecting them to read my mind? Am I helping them understand me?* Just say what you're feeling. Try to verbalize it. You're helping your spouse help you, and really, you're helping your relationship in that very moment. And those growing pains can be next-level moments, where you seek insight into your spouse's mind and soul, and you help them see into yours.

It's helpful also to take a breath and in that moment ask God for His perspective. Then you can let your guard down and say things like, "When you said this, I felt this." Or, "I know you probably didn't mean it this way, but when you did this, it hurt me." When Jennie tells me this, it lets down the walls. It makes *me* want to respond in humility and vulnerability.

It can be a struggle not to let the feelings lead but instead to feel the feelings and then communicate. Half the time we don't know how we're feeling or why—but we try to communicate that. And when there's understanding and effort on both sides—they're wanting to understand you, and you're wanting to communicate— you've got the same endgame. The endgame is to beat this level and go to the next level together. (And then—like Jennie has already mentioned—makeup sex is really awesome. Bonus level.)

Maybe you're like Jennie and your problem is articulating how you feel. You think, *I'm at a loss for words. I don't know how to say how I'm feeling because I don't know how I'm feeling.* Maybe you're like me and you can usually describe exactly what you're feeling and why, and you can give three examples of it. Either way, the issue is figuring out how to give each other space to say what you need to say, and making sure the other knows you hear them and see them and love them.

Don't rush into a conversation when you're not ready to talk about it, and don't demand that someone be able to articulate exactly what they're feeling. Instead, give the space to listen without an "I'm going to fix it" mentality, because 90 percent of the time, they don't need you to fix it. They just need you to care about it, to listen and accept it.

As you communicate, for every bad guy you defeat, it's like the video game: You get the new whistle. You get the frog. You get the reward. And you get to collect those things that make you stronger in your marriage, that keep you from slipping off the road. Treasure those things you collect as you level up together.

BRING IT HOME

- What is your communication style when you're facing conflict? Do you get tongue-tied? Do the words flow easily?
- How might the two of you accommodate your communication styles? If one (or both) of you struggles, how can you give more space and more grace?
- What are the little tools blinking in the corner of your screen that you've gotten from winning previous "big bad guy fights"? Maybe it's knowledge of each other, ways to diffuse situations, quick solutions, or problem solvers.

CONVERSATION STARTERS

- "One thing I've noticed about your conversation style in a charged environment is _____. Knowing that levels us up because _____."

WHEN WE'RE FIGHTING, WE'RE NOT FIGHTING AGAINST EACH OTHER; WE'RE ON THE SAME TEAM.

IF WE CAN MAKE IT THROUGH THAT FIGHT, WE CAN MAKE IT TO THE NEXT LEVEL IN OUR RELATIONSHIP.

- "Something I appreciate about the way you listen and communicate with me is _____. That really helps because _____."
- "I remember a game-changing communication session when you blew my mind / gave me a revelation by telling me something critical for our relationship: _____. Here's what that taught me about you/me/us _____."

PRAYER

Lord God, thank You for being the One who takes us deeper in our relationship with You, and You're the One who brings us deeper with each other as we follow You. Thank You for bringing us to new levels of intimacy, vulnerability, and communication as time goes by in our marriage. Please help us grow stronger and to cherish the tools we've gathered along the way. In Jesus' name, amen.

Don't repay evil for evil. Don't retaliate with insults when people insult you. Instead, pay them back with a blessing. That is what God has called you to do, and he will grant you his blessing.

1 PETER 3:9 NLT

CHAPTER 28

BOOSTER SHOTS

LEVI

Recently we were talking with our kids about getting flu shots. It's hard to convince them of the necessity of getting stuck with a needle. They're like, "How is a needle going to help me not get sick? I don't want to get a needle. I'd rather get sick."

We had to explain that, with asthma in our family, we are more at risk of the flu leading to a major respiratory infection flare-up, and so it's something we have to take seriously. Lenya, our second-born daughter, went home to be with Jesus after a serious asthma attack, and I have ended up in the intensive care unit with an IV in my arm, struggling to breathe, multiple times in my life. "That's much, much worse than a single poke from a needle," I explained. After hearing my very intense explanation, they were okay with it all of the sudden—not happy—but okay with it.

In 1 Peter 3, we have the marital equivalent of a full panel of booster shots—comprehensive preventative medicine. If you take these spiritual booster shots today, you're going to avoid a lot of misery down the road. In today's verse, the first shot is this: *act like you're on the same team*. That can be hard to do, right?

When you are at odds with and defending yourselves against each other, hearing that can sting a little. But it's better than getting twenty needles of marriage pain later on.

Jennie and I have to remind ourselves *continuously* that we are on the same team and that we've got to act like it. Sometimes we've got to love even when we don't like each other. We've got to choose to commit. We've got to act like we're on the same team, even when it's hard. Part of that team mindset is coaching.

When you're on the same team but you're playing against each other, sometimes one of you needs to step in and be the coach. You can say something like, "Actually, I just need you to hold me and tell me it's going to be okay. I don't need you to fix it right now."

All of a sudden, you're both back in. You're giving the other person the tools they need to fight fair since you're on the same team. You would never give your opponent a game-winning strategy. But if you're on the same team, you give each other the helpful tips, so you both win.

If you tell your spouse what you need, they can lovingly respond. Chances are your spouse would love to give what you need. They just have no clue what that is.

It can be even more difficult when *you* don't even know what you need. So when you're in that spot, really try to think it through. Ask yourself, *What would be helpful for my better half to know about what's going through my mind right now?*

Here's a second booster shot for you: *don't retaliate; compensate.* The reality is, some days, I'm not the husband I should be to Jennie. And some days, Jennie is not the wife that she wishes she were to me. On our bad days we can be hostile toward one another, and it can be tempting for the one on the receiving end to reflect back that hostility. But our goal instead should be to say, "Okay, they're not giving grace. So I'm going to give twice as much grace. This is a day where they're weak, so I'm going to be strong." And that goes against everything in our bones, but it's exactly how God rolls and how He leads us to live.

What we need to realize is that the authority to do exactly what we feel, to retaliate, is like the ring in *Lord of the Rings*. It will turn us into Gollum. It will destroy us. But when we feel vindicated for being rude because of what our spouse is doing, that's the time to throw that ring in the volcano and die to ourselves a little bit. In dying to ourselves, we're going to find life and strength. Jesus showed us this. He "did not come to be served, but to serve, and to give his life as a ransom for many" (Matthew 20:28). In losing our lives, we're going to find life. In being last, we're actually going to be first (Matthew 20:16). Don't retaliate. Compensate.

These two things, team-playing and compensating, can save your marriage a lot of grief. Trust us. It's really good medicine.

BRING IT HOME

- When do you feel like you're playing on opposing teams? What are a few ways you could coach each other and give a game-winning strategy?

- What can you do when you want to tell each other what you need but you don't know what you need? When has that happened? How'd you work through it?

- Has getting stuck in the retaliation mindset ever led you to behaviors you're not proud of? Once the hippocampus (in the brain) gets hijacked, it's all lizard brain, and the prefontal cortex is not great at making wise relational choices. What are the benefits of doubling down on compensation instead?

SOMETIMES WE'VE GOT TO LOVE EVEN WHEN WE DON'T LIKE EACH OTHER.

CONVERSATION STARTERS

- "One time that you coached me effectively was _____. I like how that worked. How can I be a better team player in times like this? Coach me, please."
- "One time that I felt baffled and didn't know what to do in a conflict was _____. Retroactively, how would you coach me?"
- "The last time I felt like retaliating was _____, because _____. Instead, a good compensation might be _____."

PRAYER

Father God, thank You for the preventative spiritual medicine You've put in Your Word. Thank You for caring that we should play and win together instead of retaliating and hamstringing ourselves. Help us welcome and respond to Your coaching and each other's. In Jesus' name, amen.

You should be of one mind. Sympathize with each other. Love each other as brothers and sisters. Be tenderhearted, and keep a humble attitude. . . . "If you want to enjoy life and see many happy days, keep your tongue from speaking evil and your lips from telling lies."

1 PETER 3:8, 10 <small>NLT</small>

CHAPTER 29

HEART TENDERIZER

LEVI

I n his epic marriage advice chapter in 1 Peter 3, Peter gives us some major caution signs and rerouting directions. These are the things that are blinking at us on the slippery road and direct us on how to traverse tricky terrain in a safer way.

Today's verses start with a basic concept: *be of one mind.* Talk about being on the same team. Having one mind, trying to think more together than separately—that is unity, and unity brings confidence and strength to a relationship. We have to protect the unity in our marriages because division saps strength. The Bible says, "How good and pleasant it is when God's people live together in unity!" (Psalm 133:1). It's good and it's pleasant, and when you have unity in your marriage, it gives you courage. If unity has somehow broken down in your marriage because trust has been broken, or if you've just let division get a foothold, it's not too late to start building unity right now.

The next concept we see in today's verses is *sympathy.* This is a powerful tool. The word translated as *sympathize* in 1 Peter 3:8 literally means "fellow feeling" or "having compassion."[1] We can have compassion for our spouses. And we can start by asking God for the eyes to see our spouses the way He does—asking Him to help us feel what they feel, to see life from their perspective.

When we start to feel less understanding and more demanding, we say things like, "Don't you care what I've been through or how I feel?" That's an indicator that something is up in our souls. If we can stop ourselves in our tracks and think something like,

Well, they're going through it too, things can change. It helps me to remember: *Hey, it's not easy to be my wife*. We were talking the other day, and Jennie said to me, "Sometimes you give me whiplash," not because I drive badly, but because I live with so much intensity and constant movement.

It helped me to see our life together through her eyes. She told me, "You realize that we've been on like ten planes in the past three weeks? And we've given seven messages? And gone to this and this and this, dinners and events and meeting people? Sometimes it's hard to keep up with it all." That was a wake-up call. I needed to slow down and relate to that. Anything we can do to find common ground and to empathize with each other is going to help our marriage greatly.

Peter reminded us in today's verses that sympathy sometimes comes by not saying what you want to say. "If you want to enjoy life and see many happy days, keep your tongue from speaking evil and your lips from telling lies" (1 Peter 3:10 NLT). Basically, Peter was saying to bite your tongue. That may sound a little harsh, but it's really good advice. Sometimes we just need to hold back and not say everything we feel, which I'm learning too. How many nights have ended up icier than they should have because I didn't bite my tongue?

If in doubt, don't say it. Just don't go there. You have the power in a marriage to hurt each other. You know each other's secrets, and you could take each other out with a sentence—with a word—because you both know the Sasquatch within. You both know how to bring that bad boy out.

You know each other's insecurities. You know where the skeletons are buried. In a marriage with any healthy amount of vulnerability,

IT'S NOT TOO LATE TO START BUILDING UNITY.

UNITY BRINGS
CONFIDENCE AND STRENGTH
TO A RELATIONSHIP.

you've given each other power to do harm, but you're trusting that because of what's written on their soul, they won't use that power against you.

That's where the real living comes.

Sometimes the Holy Spirit will say things like, *Don't say that.* He'll nudge you to be kind and trustworthy. To do that, you'll need to stay soft, tenderhearted, merciful, and easily moved to sympathy or compassion toward your spouse. In today's verses, Peter said, "Be tenderhearted, and keep a humble attitude" (v. 8 NLT). Try to cultivate that tenderness, that sweetness that you had at the beginning—when you were hanging on their every word and examining their face, trying to see if they were happy or not, when you were trying to learn to read them and know them. It took a lot of focus back then, and it will now too. Sometimes when you're in a marriage, whether or not you've been in it for a long time, you start going through the motions and lose touch with the passion and excitement of the first moments you met. Keep it tender, and keep it fresh.

Here's something else to remember: you can choose to show your spouse tenderness even when you don't feel like it.

Love is a verb. If love were a noun, then it would be just a feeling—there simply would be no love when you didn't feel like it or if they weren't acting lovable that day. But if love becomes a verb, you can love at any time. You can access that tender heart, because you've kept it tenderized.

That's a game-changer. That's a marriage-changer. That's a life-changer. Fight for tenderness so you can stir up the feelings deep inside, and decide you're going to do it whether you feel like it or not.

BRING IT HOME

- Individually, try putting yourself in each other's shoes. Try to feel what your spouse must be feeling from what they're going through. Think about what it's like to be married to you right now. What does that reveal? How might that change how you treat each other?
- When's a time you wish you'd bitten your tongue? What happened? Did you have a warning in your spirit beforehand? How can you become more responsive to that sort of wisdom?
- When have you treated each other with tenderness, you to them and them to you? How do you show that to each other most effectively, in a way that touches your hearts?

TRY A LITTLE TENDERNESS

Sit down together and recount some times you made each other's hearts pitter-patter. Maybe it was an early date, your wedding, or some sweet moments in the recent past. Describe in detail the picture you're seeing in your mind's eye as you share your memories, and really press into it. Stir up those mushy feelings. They can be fuel for tenderizing your heart. Do this regularly to keep things nice and soft, and sympathy will be easier to access.

PRAYER

Holy Spirit, guide us as we treat each other with sympathy and empathy. Help us remember to try to see life from each other's eyes. And help us have ears to hear Your voice as You lead us in the way of compassion and tenderness. In Jesus' name, amen.

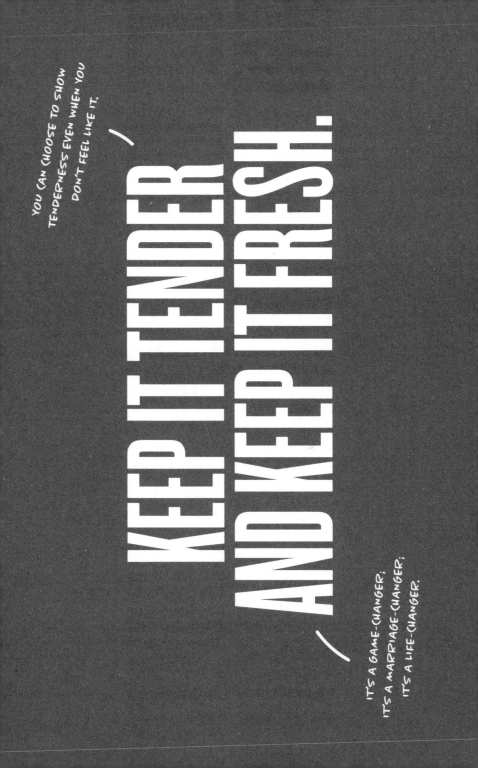

YOU CAN CHOOSE TO SHOW TENDERNESS EVEN WHEN YOU DON'T FEEL LIKE IT.

KEEP IT TENDER AND KEEP IT FRESH.

IT'S A GAME-CHANGER, IT'S A MARRIAGE-CHANGER, IT'S A LIFE-CHANGER.

LOVE NOTES

First take the plank out of your own eye,
and then you will see clearly to remove the
speck from your brother's eye.

MATTHEW 7:5

CHAPTER 30

EYE CLINIC

LEVI

We're going to cover some basic eye health today. Eyes are, after all, one of the most complex human organs, and they are shockingly vulnerable. You've heard the advice not to stare at the sun, to get regular checkups if you wear glasses, and to change your contacts. Jesus would add: avoid letting large foreign objects hang out of your own eyeballs, especially if you are about to clean a little something out of your beloved's delicate eyes.

When a firework shot in my eye in the summer of 2020, I was in excruciating pain. I was concerned that I would never see out of my left eye again and that I would have to wear an eye patch while preaching. On and on my worries went. It was a really traumatic night, and seeing Jennie (out of my good eye) driving me seriously and intensely to the same ER where our daughter Lenya went to heaven will always be seared in my mind. I learned a lot more about how eyeballs worked when that happened than I ever really wanted to know. But suffice it to say, eyes are delicate, complicated, and *full of nerves*. You do not want to go messing with them without sufficient knowledge and training.

In Matthew 7:5, Jesus said before you try to get a speck out of someone else's eye, check and see if there are any two-by-four planks sticking out of your own. Basically, He was saying, consider the firework in your eye before approaching your spouse to point out the little bit of dust in theirs.

There are days when you need to say hard things to your

spouse. This has the potential of erupting like a volcano. Think Mentos and Diet Coke. So what can you do before you approach? *Consider yourself.*

Jennie is good at saying, "Hey, this will be a hard conversation," and picking the right time. She tries to get the situation perfectly set. Someone has got the kids, and we both have time to talk, so when we're going to have a hard conversation we are good to go. But before you deliver the Mentos—"Hey, will you please stop this or that?" or "When you spend money like this without talking to me, it frustrates me"—make sure you are not also bringing Diet Coke. Meaning, make sure you're not going to cause a harmful reaction because of what's going on with you.

In Jesus' metaphor it's removing the plank from your eye before wiping out someone else's. And I don't think that with the plank/speck comparison He meant your sin is worse than theirs. If you're doing it right, your sins, to you, should look like a plank because they're so close to your field of vision.

If I had a speck in my eye right now, it would appear to me like a plank, if I were looking at it. But if I chose to look past it to my wife's, I would think I could get her speck out. But the reality is I should consider myself—*What am I not doing right? How am I letting her down?*—before I ever have the audacity to initiate a hard conversation with her about something she's doing. Plus, imagine having a plank in your eye and trying to get close enough to help someone with their dusty eye; people are going to get knocked over.

Once the planks are out, it's vital to restore the health of our eyes toward each other. We've got to look for beauty. We will see more of what we stare at. Have you ever closed your eyes after playing *Tetris* for a while? Those little squares got burned into your retinas. They might even find their way into your dreams. You see them because you stared at them all day. (That's not great for your eye health either, by the way.) You could easily spend your day finding the faults of your spouse and staring at them until they burn themselves into your brain. Or you can choose to look for and find the good. It's possible to search for beauty and to find it.

It's really easy to find the negative, isn't it? We don't have to put any energy or effort into finding the faults of others. Those things tend to take center stage right away.

But to look for the good? To look for the beauty? That takes a different kind of vision, a healthy point of view, a better kind of lens. We have to focus and look for things that we can encourage. As you start to find the beauty in your spouse, you'll be training your eyes to see more and more of it. And you'll be able to see both yourself and each other more clearly, in the way God sees you.

BRING IT HOME

- When have you experienced a plank-in-the-eye situation, when one of you showed up for a hard conversation with the explosive combo of Mentos and Diet Coke? How could that have been avoided?
- What would the ideal scenario for a "hard conversation" be for you? How would you work together to set it up?
- What good could come right now from considering how you might be letting the other person down? How can you continually do this and broach this in conversation, to keep the planks out of your eyes?

AS YOU START TO FIND THE BEAUTY IN YOUR SPOUSE, YOU'LL BE TRAINING YOUR EYES TO SEE MORE AND MORE OF IT.

YOU'LL BE ABLE TO SEE BOTH YOURSELF AND EACH OTHER MORE CLEARLY, IN THE WAY GOD SEES YOU.

VISINE FOR YOUR MARRIAGE

- Arrange a hangout at a café or at home, wherever you can give each other a good stare and find the beautiful. One of you go first: "I find it beautiful about you that _____." And then take turns. See if you can build off each other and keep the beautiful things going.
- Try to leave the conversation with at least three things you can encourage about each other in the coming week.
- Whenever your spiritual eyes start getting red and agitated, and you start getting annoyed by the negative in your spouse, haul out the eye drops and choose to see the beautiful.

PRAYER

God, thank You for caring about the health of our vision for each other. Let us keep anything log-like from obscuring our sight as we communicate, and train our eyes on the beautiful in each other. Amen.

All these blessings shall come upon you and overtake you, if you obey the voice of the LORD your God.

DEUTERONOMY 28:2 ESV

CHAPTER 31

LUCKY
IN LOVE

JENNIE

Would you consider yourself "lucky in love"? There are some people who don't like the word *lucky*. But I want to show you something beautiful about that word.

Levi interviewed a writer named Winn Collier, who wrote the official authorized biography of the late Eugene Peterson, the man and legend who gave us *The Message* version of the Bible.

In his book, *A Burning in My Bones: The Authorized Biography of Eugene H. Peterson,* Winn writes that when Eugene had finished translating the Beatitudes, the editor loved what he read—with one exception.

> Rather than using *blessed*, Eugene inserted *lucky*—not a bad translation of the Greek word *makarios*, whose meaning carries "fortunate" as well as "blessed." . . .
>
> "You can't use *lucky*," the editor explained. "There's a whole world of Texans out there who think *lucky* is the code name for Lucifer. And a whole other group who think *lucky* is an evil word denying God's providence. We'd lose a chunk of our audience." Eugene picked up the phone. "Rick, they're taking away my *lucky*. You got to get it back in there." Ultimately, Eugene surrendered, though he smuggled *lucky* in a few places of the Bible elsewhere. Eventually he got his way, though, with his volume of poetry based on the Beatitudes he called *Holy Luck*."[1]

I love this tension between *blessed* and *lucky*. Peterson was trying to say that our word *blessed*—blessed are those who mourn, blessed are those who are persecuted, blessed are those who hunger and thirst for righteousness—is not a big enough word. It doesn't convey the feeling of, *I can't believe this would happen to me! I am so lucky, lucky, lucky.*

I believe that God wants us to see that in our marriages. We can get to this place of feeling lucky—spoiled rotten by God's sweetness—if we are willing to fight to honor each other, do the hard work, love well in the little things, and keep showing up through conflicts. Diet and exercise aren't fun, but I imagine having abs is. (I don't think I've ever had defined abs.) So it is in marriage. Hard? Yes. Worth it? Totally. If you are willing to do what other people won't, you can enjoy what other people don't.

Many people get caught off guard by the difficulty and fighting in marriage. And because it's not easy, they decide to leave the relationship. But we have to remember that there can be joy and strength and power unlocked if we can work through it and keep giving and loving and respecting through the struggle. It's like the old saying—you can create your own luck.

Sociologists say about unpleasant marriages that if you keep pushing on—if you persist and take the wise, right steps to keep working on a marriage—most marriages that feel bad today will become better within five years.[2] They can become enjoyable if you just keep going.

It's possible to get to a peaceful place. I want to speak life over you and your marriage and remind you that though it's not easy to move through conflict and fighting, there is a possible reward and payoff if you just keep going and choose the next right thing.

Eugene Peterson's translation of Proverbs 21:21 says, "Whoever goes hunting for what is right and kind finds life itself— *glorious* life!" (MSG). Again, he has it right! If we're hunting and searching for the right things in the midst of conflict, we will find the glorious life—the full, abundant life Jesus came for us to live. When we're hunting or fishing, persistence overtakes us. Am I right, you outdoor sports people? We know that the reward is holding a huge trout (and making it look even bigger by stretching it toward the camera), and if we sit still long enough, we'll spot that buck we paid the tag for.

Keep working at your marriage, and you will soon look up at your spouse and think, *How did I get so lucky?* And with a smile and smirk, you'll know exactly how you got so lucky.

You'll feel lucky and free because there's plenty of room— space to enjoy the other yet still be yourself. So often people go into marriage scared because they feel like they're going to lose who they are, their identity. Like they're just going to be sucked up in this relationship and become half a person. But there's room for two personalities in a marriage. There's room for two opinions and for two callings within a calling. There's room for God to move within whole people serving and loving Him together.

If there's only one opinion in your marriage, only ever one way of doing things, then you need to reevaluate how you're operating. God wants two leaders. Two people working things out together. Yes, it's hard for two to find peace and not get bogged down by conflict—but it's possible. You just have to remember that you're not married to someone who is perfect or perfectly compatible

KEEP WORKING AT YOUR MARRIAGE!

IF YOU ARE WILLING TO DO WHAT OTHER PEOPLE WON'T, YOU CAN ENJOY WHAT OTHER PEOPLE DON'T

YOU'LL SOON LOOK UP AT YOUR SPOUSE AND THINK, HOW DID I GET SO LUCKY?

with you; you're married to a messed-up, broken person who loves a perfect God and receives grace from Him.

You're here to join that journey of serving God with someone who's in process and has rough edges. Those rough edges are going to rub against yours and help you become smoother, faster, and stronger. And to the extent that your relationship is healthy and strong and vibrant and whole, God will pour that living water that He wants to get to this world through your relationship.

If you're in an abusive relationship, what I'm saying here does not apply to your situation. Call the police, get safe, get help.

Otherwise, if you're in a difficult place, hear this: if you persevere, I believe you can grow through it and that eventually things will feel different. That you'll hit a point where you look at your life and spouse and what God is doing and say, "Look, I'm not just blessed, I'm lucky. I'm lucky to be loved like I'm loved."

Until then, let's keep trusting God. No matter what is going on in our lives, we as believers in Jesus can say, "It is well with my soul." As we look to Him in the center of our marriages, as we look to Him in the struggles and in the conflict, as we seek His presence and love, His power and help, He will show up and not only give us what we need, but *be* everything we need. And even as we do that, I believe we can each say, "It is well with my soul" and find that peace—that holy, lucky feeling.

BRING IT HOME

- Explain a time when you've felt overwhelmed by how lucky you were. What did that feel like?

- Talk about how it feels to go hunting for something and to finally get it (could be actual hunting, shopping, or anything that you need patience to look for).
- When you look at the two of you, how do you see two people's rough edges smoothing each other out in conflict? How is that something to feel lucky about?

A GAME OF LUCK

- Grab a pair of dice, pack of cards, or a spinner from a board game. Whoever rolls, casts, or spins the highest number gets to tell the other person, "I feel lucky to have you because _____." After a little while, you'll start to realize that the fact you're together is more than just dumb luck. You've been blessed by a God who knows you, and He knows exactly what you need.

PRAYER

Lord God, You are the Master in seeing the potential in what You created. You also show us what true patience looks like as You work with us individually and together. We look to You and can't believe the God who created the universe would love us and give us purpose and life. We are the lucky ones, and we are filled with gratitude. Help us to continue to show up and work hard and love and honor each other. Give us eyes to see the beauty of our relationship and how lucky we truly are. In Jesus' name, amen.

PART 8

HEALTH AND SOUL HYGIENE

LOVE NOTES

As for me, I will walk in my integrity;
Redeem me and be merciful to me.
My foot stands in an even place;
In the congregations I will bless the LORD.

PSALM 26:11–12 NKJV

CHAPTER 32

AS FOR ME

JENNIE

T oday we're going to talk about the significance of each person's role in a marriage—to understand the significance of *you* as an individual in your relationship. It's vital not only to see the significance of your spouse's role but also to love the significance of your own role. We want you to see what you get to be a part of in this marriage and choose to appreciate your individual role.

This connects to the truth that you can't change your spouse, but you can change yourself. No matter what is happening with your significant other, you can't change their behavior. You can change your own attitude and actions, going from sour to sweet. You are responsible only for yourself. And you can actually change the atmosphere of your marriage by doing this.

Linda Dillow wrote a book with an amazing title: *What's It Like to Be Married to Me?*[1] (I know, *ouch*. I sometimes just put the book on my nightstand as a reminder to ask myself this question.) It's easy to point a finger at your spouse, but change can really happen when you point a finger inward. My friend, Holly Furtick, wrote a study for women called *Becoming Mrs. Betterhalf*,[2] and she posed the possibility that your marriage can become stronger and better and sweeter if you choose to change yourself and focus on your role. Your spouse doesn't have to do a thing—although often as one spouse's attitude and mindset gets better, the other wants to serve more and love more too.

Amazing things happen when we ask questions like, "How

can I be the best spouse I can be? How can I, individually, be strong so I can be a help and not a hindrance in those situations that end in slippery-roads?"

You have a critical role in marriage *on your own*. Galatians 6:5 says, "Each of you must take responsibility for doing the creative best you can with your own life." That's *The Message* translation, and I love the way it's phrased. What would the "creative best" that you can do with "your own life" look like for you? What would that look like to your significant other? What effect could it have on your marriage?

When you are becoming the best spouse you can be, you will start seeing the best in your spouse and encouraging that. Colossians 3:17 says, "Whatever you do, whether in word or deed, do it all in the name of the Lord Jesus, giving thanks to God the Father through him." Imagine how taking that literally could change things for you in the responsibility you take for your own soul.

Throughout the Psalms, David used the key phrase "as for me." Sometimes he was focusing on his enemies, saying, "Man, my enemies are the worst. They're doing such awful things. But *as for me*, I will serve the Lord. But *as for me*, I will walk with the Lord." And in today's verse, David said, "*As for me*, I will walk in my integrity" (NJKV). There will come a time when each individual married person has to say, "As for me . . .," with regard to everyday behavior and spirituality.

You and your spouse can inspire, challenge, support, and encourage each other, but your spouse's relationship with Jesus is completely theirs. That spiritual relationship may go through many twists and turns and ups and downs in their lifetime. They cannot take responsibility for you spiritually, and you can't take responsibility for them. It can be a difficult thing, especially when one spouse doesn't see that. But when it comes down to it, we each have to choose our relationship with Jesus. To be satisfied with Him alone. To seek Him first above other relationships. To allow Him to meet our deepest needs that our spouses can't. When we are fully reliant on Jesus for everything, we can be in a place where we can actually show His love and kindness to our spouses. And *that* is beautiful living!

When you show the kindness and love of God to your spouse, no matter where they are at spiritually, it's a gift. You never know what is going on deep inside their heart. So keep praying, keep loving, keep investing, keep being the strongest spouse you can be. They are on a journey just like we all are. Don't give up.

As our verses today say, "As for me, I will walk in my integrity" (NKJV). I love that within the word *integrity*, we see the word *grit*. It's going to take grit—determination and courage—to keep giving and loving and respecting, no matter how our spouses live or respond.

Grit also refers to small granules or pieces of sand, and those of us who live in snowy regions know that sand or little pieces of rock can keep us from slipping on ice. Maybe we can make the decision to have the grit in our hearts to be gracious with our spouses, and we can also choose to lay out the grit before us, so we can keep our feet steady as we walk together.

We need each other, and when one of us is weak, the other can be strong, gracious, and steady—and vice versa. Let's choose to be strong for each other with grace and kindness. Decide today: as for me, let it be!

BRING IT HOME

- Think about the verse, "Each of you must take responsibility for doing the creative best you can with your own life" (Galatians 6:5 MSG). Does that inspire you to do something different? To do something differently with each other?
- When do you find yourself trying to take responsibility for each other in ways that are solely up to the individual? In what ways can you communicate better, "It's up to you, babe," and encourage the other person to do their creative best?
- How are each of you taking personal responsibility for your relationship with God?

INTEGRITY PRINCIPLES

- Separately, come up with a list of three to five principles that are important to you as you walk with integrity in your own life, as a spouse, as an individual, and spiritually, regardless of what's going on with the other person.
- Share those principles with each other.
- Discuss what you observe about your lists. Is there any overlap? Is there any divergence?
- How does understanding each other's main principles help you support each other? How does it help you let go of what is the other person's responsibility? How might this change things in your marriage?

PRAYER

Father God, I choose today to declare that, as for me, I will walk with integrity. You generously give us the courage to attempt things that seem impossible, so we look to You to build our integrity and grit. Thank You for Your grace and for redemption that comes only from You and from a life surrendered to You. Give us both courage to operate in the knowledge and understanding of our individual roles within our marriage. Thank You for Your love that makes all this possible. In Jesus' name, amen.

Physical training is of some value, but godliness has value for all things, holding promise for both the present life and the life to come.

1 TIMOTHY 4:8

CHAPTER 33

SOUL TRAINING

LEVI

B een to the gym lately? Or out running or swimming? When it comes to moving your body, what's your favorite type of exercise?

We all know exercise is good for your body. It's good for your heart. It's good for your health. It's good for your mind too. But even all these benefits last just a little while. Today's verse says athletic training, exercise, is good—it's of "some value." It's good for a short amount of time (way too short, in my opinion!). Today's verse goes on to say that godliness, or righteousness, is good for both this present, physical life and the eternal, spiritual life. This is the stuff that will survive the metabolic crash of middle age and the inevitable changes of our later years. The time we spend on godliness is going to profit us forever.

When I let exercise slip out of my routine, it's easy for everything to cascade out of control. All of a sudden I go from intermittent fasting and kale to "Just give me the honey biscuits. Get them on over here. Honey biscuits, with extra honey." When we start making allowances in one area, we tend to keep making more in others. And, as any serious physical trainer would tell you, every compromise adds up.

Paul was drawing a solid connection between physical training and training in godliness. Just as we cultivate our bodies' strength, we need to be cultivating the inner strength—the inner beauty and grit—that we need for our marriages. What does it look like to grow in this way? Well, like everything we want to get better at doing, godliness takes practice.

As we're writing this, Jennie is training for a half marathon. She turned forty (she likes telling people her age, so she's okay with it, promise), and she said she just felt like a half marathon is something a forty-year-old should do. I told her she's on her own with this, but she has been working hard. There have been days when it's freezing out and she'd rather snuggle on the couch, but she runs anyway. She has a friend who has run multiple marathons and IronWoman events, so she's getting great tips and coaching. One of the things Jennie has loved the most about this experience is the spiritual parallels. It highlights the effort, time, and patience that also should go into the life of our souls.

What if we put the same energy and care into the strengthening of our hearts and spirits? Just like with our bodies, we won't see the change right away. And it might be pretty discouraging because we may not see any real change for a while. But just like doing a hundred jumping jacks one time or taking a bunch of vitamins in one day won't make you immediately healthy or strong, reading your Bible one day and showing kindness to your spouse one time won't change you immediately. But consistency over time will do a deep work, and soon you will see fruit come out of your life—sometimes with surprising abundance. You'll start seeing fruit like the things mentioned in Galatians 5:22–23 (ESV): "love, joy, peace, patience, kindness, goodness, faithfulness, gentleness, self-control."

We find ourselves repeating a lot of sayings to our kids throughout the day, and one of them is "Let's practice patience." The kids have so many opportunities throughout the day when they can learn to be patient. I encourage myself to practice patience, too, because honestly, we all need this reminder—all the time.

We've got to be steady in building the kind of godliness that shows up in life. The days when you don't feel like you're getting anything out of it, that's okay. Just keep showing up and keep up the repetition. Keep worshiping, keep fasting, keep praying, keep asking for the Holy Spirit to give you those gifts, keep giving, even when it's hard. And then one day you're going to look at yourself and say, "Dang, I look good, right? My soul looks good. My marriage looks good. When did that happen?" In the faithfulness. Eugene Peterson has called it "a long obedience in the same direction."[1] It's perseverance. It's being able to say, "I never quit. I never gave up." Don't give up. It's working, even when you don't feel like it is.

Second Corinthians 4:16 says, "We are not discouraged. No, even if outwardly we are wearing out, inwardly we are being renewed each and every day" (ISV). As you both grow in years, I hope you can say that though your cartilage may be wearing out, your tendons are straining, your collagen is draining, and it's more difficult as you work out to stay fit, you're actually getting better and stronger and hotter. The beautiful thing is that your inward person is being renewed every day, getting better, more beautiful, more stunning, more gorgeous on the inside. That's the best part of growing old together, right?

BRING IT HOME

- When have you seen a certain practice change your body over time? What about inwardly—in your soul? How did it work? How long did it take?

CONSISTENCY OVER TIME WILL DO A DEEP WORK, AND SOON YOU WILL SEE FRUIT COME OUT OF YOUR LIFE.

- What would it look like to take annoying situations and look at them as opportunities to "practice patience"? Individually? With each other?
- What godly practices (like worshiping, praying, studying, giving, fasting, pursuing the Spirit) would you like to up your "reps" in? How can you make sure you're doing something every day to grow in godliness? Remember—godliness has eternal benefits and present benefits in your marriage.

MOVE IT, MOVE IT

Studies show that exercising with your partner makes your relationship stronger.[2] So this week, test that out. Ride bikes (carefully, please—learn from us!), go jogging, go to the gym, play tennis, shoot hoops together—whatever you both like to do. Notice how sharing the task of exercise changes it and makes it better. How could you share in helping each other build the muscles of godliness going forward?

PRAYER

God, we know the best things can happen over time. Show us how to gain strength not only in our bodies but in the things that last forever, so we can be strong for You and for each other. In Jesus' name, amen.

Your beauty should not come from outward adornment, such as elaborate hairstyles and the wearing of gold jewelry or fine clothes. Rather, it should be that of your inner self, the unfading beauty of a gentle and quiet spirit, which is of great worth in God's sight.

1 PETER 3:3–4

CHAPTER 34

SOUL GROOMING

JENNIE

We're about to get personal. We're going to talk grooming habits—since you've been married, you've probably learned a lot about the grooming habits of your spouse. Men, you probably had no idea how many little bottles were required to keep your lady glowing (or how much we pay for those). And ladies, you perhaps had no idea how hard it is to get whiskers out of a contact case. Or that it was possible for a human being to use the same kind of soap for every part of their body, including their hair. (What? You need at least three different kinds of washes for that.) But today we're going to dig into some biblical grooming advice.

In today's verses, Peter was talking to the ladies in the church. You women may be thinking that you are not about to take any beauty consultations from a man who lived two thousand years ago. They didn't know about retinol back then. But 1 Peter 3:3 is the timeless bit. It says, "Your beauty should not come from outward adornment." Not that it's bad to have impeccable grooming and great style. That's actually wonderful. It's fun for us to lean into what we love. If you love to wear sweats and a hat, do it. If you love to do your hair, and elaborately, awesome.

But something that I've been considering is, when I wake up in the morning, how much time am I spending to prepare my body for the day? How long does it take me to get ready?

From start to finish, it's probably an hour. I do like a luxuriously long shower. (I grew up in a small house with lots of people, so showers were timed!) This makes me think, *How does the amount of time I'm taking to prepare my outer self compare with the amount of time I'm taking to prepare my soul for the day?*

In the morning I would never go out in public without brushing my teeth. I mean, I accidentally have, and it's horrible—and I apologize if I happened to run into you on one of those few days. I also want to get the sleep out of my eyes and wash my face and put a little sunscreen on. But when it comes to our souls, how many times have we forced the world to confront a version of our souls that's not at its best? I know, it's an ouch for me too.

I always feel better starting the day when I've pampered my soul a little bit. I've had to figure out what it takes for me to be at my best, and I've learned that I just need some time, just me and Jesus in the morning. I need that peaceful time, with a cup of coffee or tea, my Bible, and a journal. If I'm not getting these things, Levi and the kids aren't getting a better version of me. Neither is anyone I'm interacting with. Every day I want to give my best and serve God with everything and shine bright in my home, community, and world with God's love.

I'm not waving a finger saying, "If you spend a certain amount of time getting your outside self ready, then you have to spend the exact same amount of time with Jesus." But it's worth thinking, *I'm putting so much effort into my outward appearance, but why am I not putting that same care and effort into my time spent in God's Word and in prayer?* When we roll out of bed, are our souls ready to face the day?

In today's Scripture passage, Peter was speaking to wives, telling them to be submissive to their husbands. He was encouraging any who had unbelieving husbands that they might lead the

NO ONE CAN BUILD UP YOUR FAITH OR YOUR LOVE FOR GOD BUT YOU.

AS YOU TAKE TIME TO BUILD UP YOUR SOUL, YOU WILL BE READY TO BUILD UP AND ENCOURAGE YOUR SPOUSE.

men to faith by simply letting their inner strength and beauty be more prominent than their outward appearance.

This is huge for us today too. Ladies, we have a special power. God has first of all given us a unique beauty, in form and figure and in the fight to honor and respect our husbands. We were built to be builders. Proverbs 14:1 says, "The wise woman builds her house, but with her own hands the foolish one tears hers down."

Peter said that husbands may be won by the behavior of their wives (1 Peter 3:1). That's an amazing superpower, to win someone over without a word. Beautiful living at its finest. And I believe God desires that for you, wife. Of course, to speak life and love and encouragement, but also to love with your actions and with the hidden person of your heart, with this incorruptible beauty. This kind of beauty is unstoppable.

Regardless of our self-care preferences, we can see from 1 Peter 3 that in order to be strong and beautiful on the inside, we must take time for soul care. Verses 20 and 21 of Jude say, "You, dear friends, by *building yourselves up* in your most holy faith and praying in the Holy Spirit, keep yourselves in God's love as you wait for the mercy of our Lord Jesus Christ to bring you to eternal life."

Both wives and husbands, no one can build up your faith or your love for God but you. So, as you take the time to build up your soul, you will be ready to build up and encourage your spouse.

BRING IT HOME

- What's your favorite kind of physical hygiene? What do you put the effort into when it comes to hair, skin, etc.?
- What about your favorite kind of soul hygiene? What kind of activities recharge you and refresh you?

- What makes your soul ready to face the world?
- What's the difference between a day when you do soul grooming and a day when you roll out of bed and get going without it? How does one or the other affect your interactions? Your decisions?
- What might happen if you whipped out the timer and decided to spend as much time on the inside as on the outside for a day? What are the benefits of this? Disadvantages?

CONVERSATION STARTERS

- "When you've had a chance to treat your soul right and get it ready for the day, I notice about you that _____."
- "My bare minimum, quick grooming routine for my physical self is _____. My bare minimum, quick grooming routine for my soul on a rushed day is (or might be) _____."
- "Like we organize our bathroom and getting-ready areas to function for us, some ways we could arrange our home to accommodate soul grooming might be _____. How can we help each other do what we need to do to treat ourselves right?"

PRAYER

Lord God, thank You for the bodies You have given us and for the ways we enjoy caring for them. We surrender to Your plan and will for us to take care of our bodies and take care of our souls. Help us see more and more the importance of building up the inner person in our hearts, so we can build up the incredible partner You have given us. In Jesus' name, amen.

Where your treasure is, there
your heart will be also.

MATTHEW 6:21

CHAPTER 35

MONEY
MATTERS

LEVI

We're going to get a little more personal here as we hone in on what tends to be a point of contention in a lot of marriages. *Finances.* It's the source of many an argument, many a discussion, and sadly, many a divorce. One survey found that "41% of divorced Gen Xers and 29% of Boomers say they ended their marriage due to disagreements about money."[1] Heartbreaking. And telling. It's easy to think that money will stop being a source of conflict if you just had more of it, but even Biggie Smalls knows that's not true. Mo' money, mo' problems.

So, *money.* What if there were a way to get on top of finances in our marriages and not let them overwhelm and suffocate us to a devastating degree? There is. It's possible to avoid having money break down our marriages and even experience great power when we let God take over our hearts and relationships with money.

Ideally, a couple would be financially wise before they even get married. In premarital meetings and counseling, there would be lots of attention given to getting out of debt, making good budget habits, saving wisely, tithing, and giving generously. But not all of us were exposed to that kind of help in the early years. Jennie and I wish we had been able to go through Dave Ramsey's *Financial Peace University* before we were married.[2] We went through it about three years into marriage, and it radically changed our minds, hearts, and habits in regard to finances. It definitely wasn't a once-for-life thing, though; "financial peace" is still a part of our marriage that we have to fight for, to be on the same page about, and to see the strength that comes from it. But it is worth the time and effort to work through it.

If money issues are plaguing you and your marriage, don't be discouraged. Let it propel you into action. It's never too late to do the right thing. It might take a while to figure things out and to see any movement, but keep fighting for it. Your lives, your marriage, your family, and the kingdom are worth it.

We can learn a lot from observing each other's money habits. If this hasn't been a part of your marriage, this will take some discussion, understanding, and vulnerability. For some of us, our money habits are tied to our upbringing and how our parents treated money. Talk to a financial counselor or financial adviser, even a financial psychologist (they're out there!). Read books. Talk about it. A great resource that discusses this subject is a book by Rachel Cruze called *Know Yourself, Know Your Money*.[3] There is help for you!

Marriage doesn't change your bad habits; it exposes them. It's like a pressure cooker bringing everything out. It's like a rock tumbler chipping off bad things and exposing what's inside. And you need the Holy Spirit there to refine and reshape you. He functions like the compounding powder in a gem tumbler—without it, those gems will chip and crack instead of getting smooth and shiny. Without the Holy Spirit, you'll get fractured, not polished.

Anything you can do that builds good money habits and good rhythms—even now—in your marriage is going to put you in a position of strength patterns (it's all about patterns!). Tithing, saving, and living on a budget are valuable decisions that can cut off future troubles at the pass.

Figuring out our history, triggers, and mindset toward finances is important. But even more necessary is our hearts' attachment to money and our views on eternity.

WE WILL NEVER GO WRONG WHEN WE PUT GOD FIRST.

WE GIVE GOD THE FIRST AND BEST, AND THAT INVITES HIM TO BLESS THE REST.

"Where your treasure is, there your heart will be also." In the passage of Scripture where our verse today sits, Jesus was sitting on a mountain with His disciples teaching them, "Do not lay up for yourselves treasures on earth, where moth and rust destroy and where thieves break in and steal, but lay up for yourselves treasures in heaven, where neither moth nor rust destroys and where thieves do not break in and steal. For where your treasure is, there your heart will be also" (vv. 19–21 ESV).

Right before Jesus said all this, He spoke about serving others, praying, and fasting. Jesus told His disciples to not be like the hypocrites, who serve, pray, and fast to be seen by others, but to do those things in the secret place. "Your Father, who sees what is done in secret, will reward you" (v. 4). Jesus was teaching His disciples what true treasure is. And it seems to be all about the heart. Not about what others see. Not about what's here on earth. There is a deeper treasure. Where our treasure is, there our hearts will be also.

Tithing and generosity allow us to be a part of the kingdom in a special way. We give the first tenth of our income to God, which is a practice that started in the Old Testament. We give God the first and best, and that invites Him to bless the rest.

When Jennie and I were first married, there were years when it was hard to tithe. Often tithing didn't make sense in our budget, but when we took that step of obedience to give God the first tenth of whatever we made, we were honoring Him. And over the years as we've continued this practice, we have seen God provide.

We will never go wrong when we put God first. I'd much rather have 90 percent of my money with God's blessing than 100 percent of it without Him. Malachi 3:10–12 says,

"Bring the whole tithe into the storehouse, that there may be food in my house. Test me in this," says the LORD Almighty, "and see if I will not throw open the floodgates of heaven and pour out so much blessing that there will not be room enough to store it. I will prevent pests from devouring your crops, and the vines in your fields will not drop their fruit before it is ripe," says the LORD Almighty. "Then all the nations will call you blessed, for yours will be a delightful land," says the LORD Almighty.

God honors the ones who honor Him. He blesses the ones who obey Him. And I want to live a life before God that honors Him and obeys Him.

Loving what God loves starts in our hearts. We love God first, and He takes care of everything else. As Jesus said in his sermon in Matthew 6, we don't need to worry about food or clothes; God knows what we need.

It's the same with our finances. When we steward well what God has given us and walk in obedience to Him, we're letting Him grow our hearts for the kingdom. We then get to see Him work in and through us in ways we never thought possible. "The world of the generous gets larger and larger; the world of the stingy gets smaller and smaller" (Proverbs 11:24 MSG).

Our prayer for you is that your world would get larger and larger together. That you, as a couple, would communicate and come to an agreement about where your treasure is and how to treat your treasure on earth. As you honor God in your finances, in tithing and in generosity to build His kingdom, your heart will be where your treasure is. And *that* is next-level living.

GOD <u>HONORS</u> THE ONES WHO HONOR HIM. HE BLESSES THE ONES WHO OBEY HIM.

AND THAT IS NEXT-LEVEL LIVING!

BRING IT HOME

- How would you describe your "money rhythms" of earning, spending, saving, tithing, investing, etc.? Are they healthy? Do you communicate openly about them? Could they be healthier in some areas?
- How do the two of you approach money differently?
- In the area of finances, do you see any potential slippery patches that need a stronger grip? How might you invite the Holy Spirit into those areas?

CONVERSATION STARTERS

- "Since we've been married, one thing I've noticed or learned about myself regarding the way I handle money is _____."
- "One money habit that I brought into our marriage that I'd like to change is _____. How can we ask the Spirit's help in this?"
- "When we look at our bank statements, knowing that our treasure goes where our hearts are, it seems to me that our hearts are going _____."

PRAYER

Holy Spirit, we invite Your presence and power into this area of our lives. Lord, You know the pain and frustration in our money matters, and we ask for Your peace and Your plan to unfold in our hearts and lives as we obey You. Lead us in the freedom, health, and wholeness that only You provide. We love You, Lord, and we are filled to the brim with gratitude. In Jesus' name, amen.

The generous soul will be made rich,
and he who waters will also be watered himself.

PROVERBS 11:25 NKJV

CHAPTER 36

THE GENEROUS LIFE

LEVI

enerosity. While the concept definitely has to do with money, generosity is also simply a way of life. Our verse today highlights "the generous soul." The soul is who we are. We are not bodies with souls; we are souls with bodies. And God's design for who we are is that we would be generous and live generously.

The Hebrew word translated as "generous" in the Bible, *berekah*, means "one who blesses," or "is a gift."[1] In the dictionary this word means, "liberal in giving or sharing; unselfish; large; abundant; ample; rich or strong in flavor; fertile."[2] A soul who blesses and is liberal in giving, who is unselfish and lives a large, abundant, flavorful life—this is a generous soul, and this is who we are meant to be in life and in marriage. Generosity makes your life bigger and bigger; stinginess shrinks it down.

This reminds me of David in the Bible. Not necessarily in the marriage department—David had several wives, but that's another story for another day. (By the way, I'm thankful the Bible doesn't gloss over the sins and mess-ups of its heroes. The Bible doesn't approve of it; it just tells the truth of a godly man's life.) David comes to mind because he was generous with honor. Let's look at how that played out in his life.

The king before him, King Saul, started off great in his own story. He seemed to be strong, and he was handsome and had the look of a king (1 Samuel 10:23–24), but over time Saul proved that he didn't trust God or let Him lead in his reign. Saul also basically spent his whole kingship trying to kill David because he was jealous of him. God had even abandoned him because he stopped inquiring of the Lord and started doing things his own way (28:16). Saul was more fearful of man than of God. And he let this fear of people lead his choices.

David, meanwhile, had been a faithful servant and armor-bearer to Saul (16:21), but Saul repeatedly threw spears at him and sent armies after him. David led the life of a fugitive for most of Saul's reign. Yet when he had opportunities to kill Saul, David said he would not lay a hand on the Lord's anointed (26:11), even though David had technically been anointed as Israel's king years prior. David had a chance to kill the guy who was trying to kill him, and he refused to do so—out of honor and generosity.

After Saul died a dishonorable and sad death, David led his people in grieving and lamenting over Saul and his son Jonathan (whom David truly loved and had a deep friendship with). David even wrote a song about it and told his people to memorize it:

> Saul and Jonathan—
>> in life they were loved and admired,
>> and in death they were not parted.
> They were swifter than eagles,
>> they were stronger than lions.
> "Daughters of Israel,
>> weep for Saul,
> who clothed you in scarlet and finery,
>> who adorned your garments with ornaments of
>> gold." (2 Samuel 1:23–24)

Now that's honor.

Wait a second, though. Was David talking about the same Saul here? Jonathan was definitely loved and admired. But Saul? Not quite. He was a man out of control, obsessed with himself and his kingdom. And what did David see? Whatever he saw and experienced of Saul, he ultimately knew that Saul had been anointed king by God. For that reason, David would not lift a hand against him.

David's honor for a bad king is astounding. It's counterintuitive. I would say it is weird and not normal. But it's also generous. It's almost like he went overboard in Saul's praises. He knew what God wants us to know: regardless of how we are treated, we can be generous in honor toward others. Honor has nothing to do with someone earning it; it has everything to do with honoring the person God created, honoring the fact that God made that person in His image.

We can be generous in honor and respect not only for the sake of another person but also for the posture of our own hearts and minds. Honor for others changes us in the process.

In marriage we can be generous in honor and respect. Perhaps our spouses have broken our trust. I am not making light of that. The pain from that is real and deep. But if we can come to a place where we see the design of God in our spouses, we see who God made them to be and their potential, we can speak to the king or queen inside them, not the fool (even if the fool is more obvious and in charge at the moment).

In marriage we need to fight to be intentionally generous with our spouses. This has a lot to do with the language our spouses speak. What is their love language? (If you haven't read Gary Chapman's *The Five Love Languages*, this will greatly help you.[3] And another book by Chapman called *The Four Seasons of Marriage* will help you too.[4]) Sometimes we try so hard to show love to our spouses, but we're giving that love in the way we want to receive it. Our spouses may be craving acts of service, but we keep giving them words of affirmation, telling them we love them. That's not bad, but maybe what would really fill up your spouse would be doing the dishes. We have to work on being generous to our spouses in their love language.

We also can grow in being generous through our tone and body language. Eye contact is huge. For me, it's resisting the urge to write a chapter of a book in my head while Jennie's telling me things. It's not framing what I'm going to say next or what I'm going to do after the conversation. This means a lot to her, so I try to be intentional and focused so I can get better at it.

Generosity is also sacrifice. It's knowing, *What is it going to mean to her if I do this little thing? If I pick up the bedroom, if I offer to put the kids to bed so she can have a little bit of Jennie time, what will that mean to her?* It's being generous intentionally, creatively, and not just selfishly giving how you want to give love.

Being generous takes work and intentionality. It takes focus and thinking differently. You ask yourself,

How would what I'm doing affect them?

What would really bless them?

Do they want to hold hands, even if I'm not that into holding hands? I can do that.

I love those little notices. We've mentioned already that sex starts in the kitchen, and basically that means that your tone and tenderness outside the bedroom makes an impact on the intensity in the bedroom. It's all connected—especially for the wife. A tender, nonsexual touch could be the greatest turn-on for your wife. (Just trying to help a brother out here.)

It helped me to realize that Jennie's flourishing should be my priority because I'm her husband. And literally, a *husband* is a technical term for a gardener who tends to a vine. So the farmer gives the vine a husband (*husbandry*), who in turn gives the vine what it needs to flourish and be at its best.

That's different season by season and day by day. It takes communication and learning what's on your spouse's schedule, what they're carrying, what they've had to deal with that day, so you can adjust your approach.

Honestly, our marriage didn't start this way. This didn't come naturally to me. Jennie will testify. But things have changed. It comes with practice. If you're not practicing generosity and attentiveness in your marriage, you can start now. Just know that improvement is going to take time because you're planting seeds.

As you plant seeds of intentional generosity, you will find that as you bless, you are blessed; as you give, you will receive; as you water, you will be watered. The generous life is beautiful living at its finest.

BRING IT HOME

- How do you each receive love? In what ways do you differ or overlap? (if you haven't yet, it could be super helpful to take a love language quiz!)
- How would you describe the levels of generosity and attentiveness in your lives right now? When have they been at their highest?
- How good are you at listening to each other? When do you feel really listened to? When do you know your spouse is not

THE GENEROUS LIFE IS BEAUTIFUL LIVING AT ITS FINEST.

IT TAKES WORK AND INTENTIONALITY.

IT TAKES CREATIVITY AND SACRIFICE.

IT TAKES FOCUS AND THINKING DIFFERENTLY.

listening? And what about the other way around—when do you find yourself engaged or not engaged in listening?

CONVERSATION STARTERS

- "I feel really loved and seen when _____. And I feel unseen and overlooked when _____."
- "Things I think you might enjoy, or things that I could do to bless you, might be _____. Can you correct me and guide me to what would make a difference for you?"
- "A few small notices or attentive actions that might make a huge difference for me are _____."

PRAYER

Lord God, thank You for showing us what true generosity is by giving us the gift of Your only Son, Jesus. You have freely given to us, and we want to grow in freely giving to others, especially each other. We choose to exchange selfishness for generosity. Open our eyes and make us aware of and attentive to each other so we can refresh each other and help each other flourish. Thank You for Your goodness that gives us the strength and motivation to grow and stay fresh. We praise You. In Jesus' name, amen.

PART 9

OBEDIENCE AND SUBMISSION ARE MORE AWESOME THAN YOU MIGHT THINK

LOVE NOTES

They said, "Let's call the young woman and ask her about it." So they called Rebekah and asked her, "Will you go with this man?"

"I will go," she said.

GENESIS 24:57–58

CHAPTER 37

I WILL FOLLOW HIM WHEREVER HE MAY GO

LEVI AND JENNIE

A few months before our family moved to Montana to start Fresh Life Church, we were hanging out with our friends Kevin and Alaina Guido in our house in California. We were discussing and dreaming about this new idea that seemed to hit us like a lightning bolt on a sunshiny day. A crazy idea to start a church. And to start a church in Montana of all places. At that point, we had visited Montana twice, and still we weren't entirely sure about it.

Meanwhile, Kevin and Alaina (pregnant with their first child) looked at each other and both told us something that floored us. "If you guys move to Montana, we will go." The idea was nuts because they had never even been to Montana. Looking back, we laugh because we thought *we* were taking a big step of faith in saying yes, but their faith was stunning—and also terrifying. Our decision would impact our friends' lives—what if *we* were wrong?

We said yes to the Lord. And so did Kevin and Alaina. They packed all their things into a U-Haul and drove up to Montana with a completely inspiring faith. Today, fifteen years later, they are still saying yes to God in Fresh Life Church, loving Jesus, and leading well. We're so grateful to see their steps of faith along the way. It hasn't been easy, but they've been faithful, and they've just kept showing up.

In today's verses, Rebekah told a stranger, "I will go." She chose to say yes. To what, exactly? To marrying Isaac, a man she had never met. To going to a place she had never been. What kind of faith was this? Abraham had asked his servant to go where

Abraham's family was to find a wife for his son Isaac. God led Abraham's servant to Rebekah, who decided to follow God into the unknown. I believe that's what God is calling us to do.

Rebekah made this decision without having all the answers. She didn't have a road map with all the dangerous, slippery spots marked with an X. She gave the yes before she knew the details. She just resolved to go for it. She made the faith decision to follow after God and what He had for her. Rebekah took a leap, and it was incredible.

When you got married, you and your spouse took the leap to say to each other, "I choose to go with you for the rest of our lives." It may have been terrifying, it may have been exciting, but it was a step of faith down your path. Because none of us knows what the future will bring. But every day we can choose to say the same thing to each other and to God in faith: "I will go. In our marriage, in God's plan for us together, I will go."

What could it look like if we drew a line in the sand and decided that as we handle our relationships, as we move forward and nurture our friendship with our spouses with care, that we will choose to follow God, to take our cues from our King in everything? What if we purposed in our hearts to approach every relationship in our lives with that kind of resolve and faith? *Yes, Lord, I will follow You. Into the wild. Into the unknown.*

What could God have for you as you step forward in faith with a *yes* to your spouse as Rebekah did with Isaac? Where could He be leading you in marriage? In your individual or shared calling? We can confidently say, "I will go," because when we take that step of obedience with faith, we're telling God, *You lead, Lord. We are Your servants, and we will follow You wherever You lead us.*

BRING IT HOME

- Aside from saying "I do," what kinds of big-leap risks have you taken in your life? In your marriage? When have you decided, "I'm in"? What happened?

- If you got out of bed each morning, looked at each other, and said, "I will go with you," what would you be saying yes to? What effect would that kind of resolve have on what you accomplish together?

- Is God asking you to take any risks, big or small? How could you come to a place of saying, "I will go" to wherever He is leading you, not knowing what's ahead?

CONVERSATION STARTERS

- "Someone I admire who took a big risk is _____. Here's why I find them inspiring: _____."

- "Metaphorically, where are you going in faith? Where could you use some company? How can I come with you? When you go to _____, I will go."

- "In the past I've felt God leading me to _____, and I said yes even though I wasn't sure. Here's how that worked out: _____."

PRAYER

Yes, Lord, to wherever You lead us. The lovely road, the hard road, we will follow You. As we move forward in our marriage together, we will choose to follow You, to take our cues from You in everything.

We want Your will to be done and Your name to be glorified. You are God in heaven and we are here on earth, so we will let our words be few and listen to You. Even if we can't see what's ahead when You call us, together we will say, "I will go." In Jesus' name, amen.

LOVE NOTES

Wives, in the same way submit yourselves to your own husbands so that, if any of them do not believe the word, they may be won over without words by the behavior of their wives, when they see the purity and reverence of your lives. . . .

Husbands, in the same way be considerate as you live with your wives, and treat them with respect as the weaker partner and as heirs with you of the gracious gift of life, so that nothing will hinder your prayers.

1 PETER 3:1–2, 7

CHAPTER 38

IN THE SAME WAY

JENNIE

T oday's verses are powerful. When we lean into the way God means for us to engage with them, they can bring great strength and confidence in our marriages. These verses can also be misused or misunderstood, causing our eyes to widen, our throats to clench. But let's look a little deeper into God's Word and see how He wants to lead our thoughts when it comes to words like *submit* and *weaker partner*.

These words have been used to make women feel less-than, but it's important to know that the culture in which they were written functioned in a far different way than ours. These things are worth understanding, and God desires for us to embrace the treasure that is in this passage.

Let's start with the words "in the same way" (v. 1). In the same way as what? In the same way as Jesus. Warren Wiersbe said, "If both partners will imitate Jesus Christ in His submission and obedience and His desire to serve others, then there will be joy and triumph in the home."[1] Within marriage, there is a goal for us to be a picture of Christ's love for the church and to be a picture of the gospel for all who see it.

That's why we're beginning with the repeated phrase "in the same way." Wives, in the same way. Husbands, in the same way. Which way is it? *The same way.* What's the same way? The answer is the way Jesus lived—which was not for His own sake but for Heaven's sake (2:23–25). Jesus submitted to God, to the point of death, to save us from our sins and from death. He submitted to

WE WANT TO DO
THINGS IN THE SAME WAY
THAT JESUS DID.

WITHIN MARRIAGE, THERE IS A GOAL FOR US TO BE A PICTURE OF CHRIST'S LOVE.

the Father out of love. We want to do things *in the same way* that Jesus did. Don't live for your sake. Live for Heaven's sake.

That's what Jesus modeled. His spirit was to submit to His Father's will, as He demonstrated so intensely in the garden of Gethsemane before He was arrested and went to the cross. "Father," He prayed, "if it is Your will, take this cup [of suffering] away from Me; nevertheless not My will, but Yours, be done" (Luke 22:42 NKJV). That's submission. The Jesus way.

LEVI

In today's passage Peter pivoted to relationships, but he kept the image of the submissive Jesus in mind. Peter was saying, "Wives, be just like Jesus. Live in the same way as Jesus. Follow His lead. Imitate Jesus in marriage." Then he talked to husbands. "Husbands, figure out where your wife is weak. She's the weaker partner in some ways, but so are you."

Think about it like this. A Ford truck is stronger than a Lamborghini in some ways, and a Lamborghini is stronger than a Ford truck in other ways. You want to race across the country? Lambo it is. A woman is like a Lamborghini. Complex. Detailed. Delicately strong. Beautiful. You're not going to take that thing off-roading. So men, in that way your wife's the "weaker" vessel. She's sophisticated. The sport car is expensive. There's the heated steering wheel and the fancy tires. You're a Ford F-150, bro. Really good for lumber, not so good with the Italian steering.

So as you follow this advice in the Bible, husbands and wives both, you're figuring out where your spouse is weak and where you're strong and how you can compensate and calibrate for each other. And when you get on the same team, you become a threat to the Enemy. You've got a truck for whenever you need a truck, and you've got a high-speed sports car for whenever you need it—so you have covered all your bases. That's a powerful thing.

Now what does this kind of submission look like? It looks like husband and wife following Jesus in everything. It looks like both of you submitting to the Lord, and letting that humility and gratitude lead the way in the approach to your relationship with each other. It's Proverbs 3:5–6 in action: "Trust in the LORD with all your heart, and lean not on your own understanding; in all your ways acknowledge Him, and He shall direct your paths" (NKJV).

Trust the Lord your God, the Designer of this universe, of you, of your spouse, and of your marriage. Depend on Him for every decision, every response, and every discussion, and He will direct your life. *That* is the best way to live!

BRING IT HOME

- How does knowing each other's weaknesses help you compensate and calibrate for each other in marriage?
- In what ways do the two of you meet in the middle, where one of you is weak in an area and the other is strong?
- What would it look like to imitate Jesus' attitude of submission, to "live for heaven's sake" in your marriage? In what situations would that be hard? Easy?

CONVERSATION STARTERS

- "You are a like a Lamborghini/Ford F-150 in that _____."
- "I am super relieved that you can help compensate for me in the area of _____, because _____. Thank you for being the stronger partner there."
- "When we're both separately getting closer to Jesus, I can tell a difference in our relationship because _____. Thanks for meeting me in the middle."

PRAYER

Lord Jesus, we want to trust You more in our own hearts and together. We surrender to Your will and choose to let You lead us in paths of righteousness for Your name's sake. In the same way we follow You, we want to approach each other with humility and kindness. Help us see each other with fresh eyes and in the same way You see us. We submit to You, Lord. In Your name, amen.

Submit to one another out
of reverence for Christ.

EPHESIANS 5:21

CHAPTER 39

THE S
WORDS

LEVI

G od gives us three tools designed to help us succeed in marriage. You can call them the three S's, if you like: *submit*, *serve*, and *study*.

To *submit* to Jesus, *submit* to your spouse.

To *serve* Jesus, *serve* your spouse.

To *study* Jesus, *study* your spouse.

These are things we can do to beautify our marriages, the inner things that can cultivate a fresh infusion of life that can flow out of our unions.

These three things not only are perfectly exemplified by Jesus but also are key for both husband and wife, though they will approach them from their own angles.

You'll remember from the last entry that in 1 Peter 3, Peter started out with the instruction for wives to "submit" to their husbands (v. 1). And in verse 7, when Peter started talking to husbands, you probably noticed he didn't use the word *submit*. Yes, true, but listen very carefully: both parties in the marriage should make it their goal to submit to each other, serve each other, and study each other.

You might be thinking, *I need a verse for that.* All right, then, I give you today's verse: "Submit to one another out of reverence for Christ." Ephesians 5 is a chapter about marriage.

So what is marriage? Marriage is two people submitting to each other.

The word translated as "submit" in this passage is the word *hupotassó* in the New Testament Greek, which means "to rank under."[1] If you rank under someone, you follow their orders. So submission in marriage is me saying to Jennie, "I want to do what's in your heart. I want to submit to you. I want to see what's in your heart be released." And it's Jennie doing the same thing to me. If we're both submitting to each other out of reverence for Christ, we're both praying about the decisions we're making. That's what's going to cause our marriage to thrive. Marriage is not one leader always telling one follower what to do; it's two leaders serving together, seeking to outdo each other in honor and in honoring Jesus as the head.

Now, what if there is a tie? This is a tough thing, because if we both get a vote, there are only two votes. What happens if it's a cat's game, like in tic-tac-toe? What do we do now? Two people voted, and you're at a fifty-fifty split. Well, in that situation the Bible says that the man should be willing to check his heart and make sure his motives are pure, and then prayerfully, before God, exercise the tie-breaking vote (1 Peter 3:7). In these eighteen years of marriage, I have never broken a tie and played that trump card. There have been *plenty* of times I wanted to, but it was always a fleshly impulse and one that, after listening to the Holy Spirit, I couldn't in good conscience go with. Consensus is the goal. Harmony. Not uniformity but unity.

If both husband and wife are seeking God's will in a situation, there will be a humility and an ease when it comes to decisions and choices that the couple needs to make. You may have found it happen the same as we have. One of us wants to do something or go somewhere, or one of us feels like God might be leading in a certain way. Usually, the other spouse's response is an easy, "Yes, let's do it," unless there is a scheduling conflict or something that

BOTH PARTIES IN THE MARRIAGE SHOULD MAKE IT THEIR GOAL TO SUBMIT TO EACH OTHER, SERVE EACH OTHER, AND STUDY EACH OTHER.

CONSENSUS IS THE GOAL!
NOT UNIFORMITY, BUT UNITY!

makes the other question if it's the best thing. Conversation and communication and sharing how we feel about something is vital in the process of deciding together.

I think the picture many of us have in our minds of the submissive wife and the husband who's a leader can turn your marriage into basically the man being Jabba the Hutt instead of Jesus the Christ. But God intends for your marriage to be like Jesus, where you're both serving each other. You're submitting to each other. You're studying each other. And you're both serving, becoming stronger in the process.

BRING IT HOME

- When you study each other and discover what's in the other person's heart, the dreams and purposes your spouse wants to release, how does that link up with submitting to each other in bringing that about? How can you better follow each other's lead to help each other thrive in that way?
- What tends to happen when you have a "tie" in your decisions? When the two of you vote differently? How does that go down?
- If you were going to "outdo each other in honor and in honoring Jesus as the head"—submitting, serving, and studying—what kinds of things would you do? How would you start the healthy competition?

TIEBREAKER

Agree on a process to implement next time there's a tie. Here's an example:

1. Pray about the issue separately and together.
2. Search your own heart, using the three *S*'s.
3. Search Scripture.
4. Get counsel.
5. Come back together and be open to compromise.

Write out your process and tack it to the fridge or somewhere you'll see it. You could even print it out and sign it. The next time you come to an impasse, see how well the three *S*'s work in action.

PRAYER

Father God, thank You for the tools You've given us in marriage. Please lead us as we submit to, study, and serve each other. Help us love and respect each other in this way as we submit to, study, and serve You. In Jesus' name, amen.

Cultivate inner beauty, the gentle, gracious kind that God delights in. The holy women of old were beautiful before God that way, and were good, loyal wives to their husbands. Sarah, for instance, taking care of Abraham, would address him as "my dear husband." You'll be true daughters of Sarah if you do the same, unanxious and unintimidated.

1 PETER 3:4–6 MSG

CHAPTER 40

STUDY UP

JENNIE

How do you feel about tests? There are a lot of different kinds of tests out there, but I'm specifically talking about the tests we took in school. My hands are sweating just thinking about it. There was just so much pressure to learn and take a test and get all the answers right—or it would impact your whole life. I love learning, but I'm thankful I'm not taking academic tests these days (though I do want to go to interior design school one day). The testing in my current life is usually the testing of my patience and the kind that God likes to insert every now and then for my growth and benefit and depth. I guess in a way we'll never actually get out of test taking. There's always a need to study up and get ready for another one.

In the previous entry we talked about the three *S*'s of marriage—*submit*, *serve*, and *study*. Today, I want to take a closer look at the third *S* word: *study*. When it comes to studying your spouse, this kind of learning and growing will help you find new depth in your marriage role. And it will help you get ready for the trying, testing times.

So when we study for marriage, what do we study? We can start with people in the Bible. In today's verse Peter said essentially, "Look to the holy women in the past. See how those women who put their hope in God made themselves beautiful. They did it by being good and loyal, like Sarah was."

If you're studying women in the Bible, you'll know that Sarah actually has a crazy story (you can read it starting in Genesis 11).

And honestly, looking at her story, you might think, *Wait. Peter was making Sarah an example of a godly wife? She made some wild decisions.* But Peter pointed to her as an example to follow, for us as wives, of honoring her husband. Sarah and Abraham weren't perfect, but they honored each other. So we study examples in the Bible—of what to do *and* what not to do.

Also, we can study examples from people around us. If you take a moment and think right now, you can probably make a quick list of marriages you look up to and want to emulate, and you can also think of examples you don't want to follow. Both are actually helpful. In the church we're surrounded by relationships. We're surrounded by marriages. Some are positive examples we can look to, so we might ask those couples, "How do you do *this*? How do you deal with *that*?" These relationships are in your family, in your community—all around you. You can look to them with a studying, learning eye and discern what to do and not to do in your own marriage. If we have the eyes to see and a curiosity, we can learn from anything and anyone.

And then, as we've said before, we study ourselves and each other. I like to keep a note on my phone titled "Being a Levi Aaron Lusko Expert." I take notes on the guy. What if, whenever your spouse mentioned something they liked or wanted to do one day, you made note of it? Becoming an expert on your spouse—that is something special.

Another incredible way to study each other is by going to professional counseling, both alone and together. It's like having a professor lead you in the study of yourself, your spouse, and the way you interact. When we enter counseling as married people, we can start looking at the baggage that perhaps we had before we even met our spouses. It's so important to get the help we need, so we're not just continuing to carry this baggage around with us everywhere we go. We're not shoving it under the carpet and pretending the earth is flat; no, we're willing to study it. We're bringing it to the surface and allowing God to heal it and to bring strength for our future so we can be the stronger, best version of ourselves for us and for our spouses.

Levi and I have both benefited from counseling—separately and together. Pro tip: when you have a counseling session, you might not want to continue the discussion during date night. Maybe in some circumstances that could be helpful, but if date nights are meant to be about enjoying each other and not necessarily talking about the hard stuff, think twice about it. Sometimes things need to get heavy and you bare your souls to each other, and sometimes you want to keep things light and fun and avoid dealing with cry-face in a restaurant. (I may or may not be speaking from experience here.) Your call—just sayin'.

However you do it, it's an amazing thing to study each other, to look at the resources around you, and gain wisdom for your marriage. All these things can help you move forward unanxious and unintimidated. What will your next topic of study be?

BRING IT HOME

- When you were young, was there someone you "studied" to learn how to be an adult? What made you pick them? Why were they your role model?
- What kinds of attributes would belong to a couple you'd want to study?

YOU NEVER KNOW WHAT GOD COULD DO IN THE WAITING.

IT'S USUALLY BEAUTIFUL, UNEXPECTED, AND MIRACULOUS.

- What are your thoughts on counseling? How have you witnessed or experienced an internal healing from the "study" of it by a professional?

BUILD YOUR CURRICULUM

Fire up your interwebs to help you identify subjects of study together:

1. *In the Bible.* Identify and list couples in Scripture you want to know more about and discover what made them tick, what commentaries say about them, and what their motivations and decisions were.

2. *In your life.* List some couples you're interested in being like, and maybe even those you want to avoid turning out like. Take notes on them. (Don't worry about being a creeper.) If you have a chance, ask if you can interview them and see what advice they have to give.

3. *Each other.* If you're not seeing a counselor, research and write down names and contacts for some qualified, certified counselors in your area. That way you have them on hand. Identify some personality tests you can take to study each other as well, such as Enneagram and StrengthsFinder. It's about as close as you can get to an instruction manual on your spouse.

PRAYER

God, thank You that we're not alone in our marriage. Thank You that You have given us good examples to follow and other examples to learn from and receive warnings from. Build our curiosity for each other and help us be aware of the little things, the little nuances and quirks of each other. We want always to be learners and students of the one You gave us to serve and love and live with. In Jesus' name, amen.

LOVE NOTES

Isaac pleaded with the LORD for his wife, because she was barren; and the LORD granted his plea, and Rebekah his wife conceived. But the children struggled together within her; and she said, "If all is well, why am I like this?" So she went to inquire of the LORD.

GENESIS 25:21–22 NKJV

CHAPTER 41

WHAT WAITING LOOKS LIKE

LEVI AND JENNIE

S ometimes life doesn't go the way we dreamed it would. Actually, life usually doesn't happen the way we think it should. When we were first married, we thought about waiting five years to have kids. It seemed like a good time frame. It would give us time to just be with each other, to enjoy being married, and to grow up a little bit more before raising tiny humans.

We can plan our ways, but God is the One who directs our steps (Proverbs 16:9). His way is so much better than what we could ever dream up or schedule for our lives. As you might have already guessed, our first child came earlier than we thought. Alivia was conceived nine months after our wedding (from some great makeup sex—sorry, not sorry, Liv) and born within the first two years of getting married. So much for the five-year plan!

If we have learned anything, we have learned that life is unpredictable. And it can take a sudden turn that will change the whole course of your life.

In today's passage, we see that Isaac and Rebekah weren't able to have kids for years. Twenty years to be exact. They met and got married when Isaac was forty, and the Bible says he was sixty when Rebekah gave birth to their twins (Genesis 25:26).

That must have been a long twenty years. Especially in a day when bearing children was viewed by the culture as a sign of blessing, and barrenness was the opposite of that.

It's interesting how the Bible can make a situation seem like it only took hours when it actually took years. In Genesis 25:20, the Bible says Isaac was forty years old when he took Rebekah as his wife. And verse 21 says, "Now Isaac pleaded with the LORD for his wife, because she was barren; and the LORD granted his plea, and Rebekah his wife conceived" (NKJV). We can imagine that from the start of their marriage they wanted children. They prayed for children. But there was a long pause between prayer and answer in these two verses. There was a time of waiting and probably frustration and pain for them both.

Are the two of you in a time of waiting? There are so many things—hopes, dreams, children, jobs, direction. It is hard to wait, but we want to encourage and remind you today to wait with His strength and His purpose in your hearts and lives.

> Have you not known?
> Have you not heard?
> The everlasting God, the LORD,
> The Creator of the ends of the earth,
> Neither faints nor is weary.
> His understanding is unsearchable.
> He gives power to the weak,
> And to those who have no might He increases strength.
> Even the youths shall faint and be weary,
> And the young men shall utterly fall,
> But those who wait on the LORD
> Shall renew their strength;
> They shall mount up with wings like eagles,
> They shall run and not be weary,
> They shall walk and not faint. (Isaiah 40:28–31 NKJV)

We can wait patiently *for* the Lord and wait *on* the Lord. We can worship while we wait. We can serve while we wait. We can love and honor and respect and get the most out of the waiting room.

You probably don't have the best experience with waiting rooms, right? The waiting room is a place where we wait to see the doctor, maybe to hear good news or bad news. The waiting room is generally a bland, clinical place where you'd never want to stay for too long, but whatever awaits on the other side of the door could change your life, one way or the other.

Whatever waiting room we find ourselves in, let's keep waiting on the Lord, trusting Him, and looking up. And let's even look out and see who else might be in the waiting room—a person God might have us encourage and listen to and speak life over. You never know what God could do in the waiting. It's usually beautiful, unexpected, and miraculous.

In Isaac we see a special reliance on the Lord in his marriage as he pleaded with God and asked for a miracle on behalf of his wife. He had waited a long time for a wife, and then God brought Rebekah to him at the perfect time (Genesis 24:67). Then when they faced this trial of waiting for children, we see them bringing their hearts' desire to their God, who had provided and made a way in the past.

It's easy to wait and worry. Worrying is a natural response to uncertainty, or to simply not having what you hope for, but it's not the recommended route. Jesus asked in Matthew 6:27, "Which of you by worrying can add one cubit to his stature?" (NKJV). To worry is to spend unnecessary energy on something we have no control over. We can choose to worry, or we can choose to watch. It's possible to watch God move in the waiting, to ask for His perspective.

WHATEVER YOUR
SEASON, GOD SEES YOU,
AND HE CARES.

IT'S POSSIBLE TO CELEBRATE WHERE YOU ARE, EVEN IN THE PAINFUL TIMES.

DEEP WITHIN
THE ACHE, THERE IS JOY
TO BE FOUND.

Let's be married couples who look up and watch what God might do in the middle of the waiting. Because nothing is impossible with God (Luke 1:37). He loves to move in our lives beautifully when things don't make sense.

Let's run to the Lord. Let's trust Him. He is in control. He knows the situation you're facing in your marriage. He knows what you're waiting for. He knows the heart of your adult child who is making poor choices. He sees your desire to have children and wants to move deeply and profoundly in your heart. He knows where this waiting room will lead and what the open door will bring. But there are lessons here in the waiting room. Don't rush the lessons. You will grow deeper and stronger. There is purpose, beauty, and wisdom to be gained—right here.

Lean into this, and keep learning to lean on your Father. He's carrying you. He will hold you. And "if any of you lacks wisdom [to guide him through a decision or circumstance], he is to ask of [our benevolent] God, who gives to everyone generously and without rebuke or blame, and it will be given to him" (James 1:5 AMP).

We want to wait wisely, in touch with God like Isaac was. And while we wait, who knows what God will do?

BRING IT HOME

- What does waiting look like in your marriage right now?
- Do you naturally worry when you wait? Where does this lead your mind?
- Do you naturally worship when you wait? Where does this lead your mind?

- What does it look like for you to plead with the Lord for a desire in your heart like Isaac did? In your spouse's heart?

PRAY THESE VERSES

- This week, write down Isaiah 40:28–31 and put it in a place where you both will see it every day.
- Ask God to increase strength in your hearts individually and together.
- Pray together as you wait for what God wants to do in your lives.

PRAYER

Lord, our everlasting God, we look to You in the waiting times. Thank You that there is strength to be found as we wait on You. Thank You that there can be purpose in the waiting room. Strengthen our hearts and minds to focus on You and to see our circumstances with Your perspective. We choose to worship You and watch, not to worry while we wait. In Jesus' name, amen.

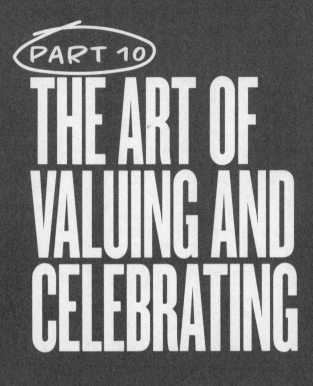

PART 10

THE ART OF VALUING AND CELEBRATING

LOVE NOTES

She gave this name to the L ORD who spoke to her: "You are the God who sees me," for she said, "I have now seen the One who sees me."

GENESIS 16:13

CHAPTER 42

YOU ARE SEEN

LEVI AND JENNIE

We experience different seasons in our lives, sometimes even seasons within seasons *Interstellar* style. Which season is it for you right now? Are you newly married? Been together for decades? Are you in a good spot? Married wishing you were single? Are you a parent wishing you weren't? Not a parent but wishing you were?

We believe it's possible not only to endure in a season but to enjoy and actually celebrate your season. It's possible to celebrate where you are, even in the painful times. This could be a season of loss and ache and struggle and frustration together. We want to acknowledge the depth and reality of this pain you might be in. If you are walking through the grief and death of someone you love, or are facing a diagnosis, or have found out the road to having children is going to be long and difficult, that is real, and that is really hard. We don't want you to think we're saying just to put up a happy celebration sign over your pain, but we are saying that deep within the ache, there is joy to be found and seen and clung tightly to. As our dear friends Jay and Katherine Wolf—who wrote some incredible books called *Hope Heals* and *Suffer Strong*—like to say, "Don't wait to celebrate."[1] We don't have to wait until things are good and going 100 percent perfectly in order to worship the Lord and celebrate His goodness.

Looking back to Genesis 16, you might remember the story of Abraham, Sarah, and Hagar. God had promised Abraham descendants beyond number, but he and his wife, Sarah, were so old they thought it was never going to happen. Like really old. Yep, older than what you might be thinking. *Old.* So they decided Abraham would have a child with Sarah's Egyptian maidservant, Hagar. Things got really messy for a while, as you might imagine. Think reality TV times ten, and you're close. Sarah had come up with the idea and tried to handle a God-sized dream with human strength, and the consequences were rough. The result? Hagar became pregnant with Abraham's baby, she despised Sarah, and Sarah couldn't handle it.

We're assuming Hagar didn't have much of a say in this arrangement. But what we do know for sure is that Sarah "dealt harshly" with Hagar (v. 6 NKJV). So Hagar, pregnant and distraught, ran away to a desert place.

Here's something beautiful though: Genesis 16:7 says, "The Angel of the LORD found her by a spring of water in the wilderness" (NKJV). Whenever the Angel of the Lord shows up in the Old Testament, that is Jesus. This was the very first time that Jesus, God in flesh, showed up to a human, and it was to Hagar, an Egyptian maidservant who was pregnant by her boss's husband.

God literally showed up for Hagar and her yet-to-be-born son, who would be called Ishmael. He spoke to her and promised her innumerable descendants, and she named that spot *Beer Lahai Roi*, "the One who lives and sees me," or "the God who sees me." Naming that spot—that was a kind of celebration of her season.

This is also the first mention of a name of God given by a human. How lovely is this? God pursued Hagar and found her, and she was seen by Him in a season of her life that she might have thought was the end for her.

Whatever your season, God sees you, and He cares. It doesn't matter who you are or what you've done, or what has been done to you. In the New Testament, Peter wrote, "Humble yourselves, therefore, under God's mighty hand, that he may lift you up in due time. Cast all your anxiety on him because he cares for you" (1 Peter 5:6–7). He's with you wherever you are.

God also saw humanity stuck in sin, and His answer was sending His Son, the Angel of the Lord, to earth, and giving Him as a sacrifice to die on the cross and rise from the dead so we could have an abundant life and hope in death. We have hope. *That's* what makes it possible to celebrate our season.

You and your spouse might not be in a season as intense and difficult as Hagar's, but regardless of the level of pain, it is still pain and heartache—and it's *your* pain and heartache. We want to remind you that God sees you.

And even more than that, God gives you the remedy. He *is* your remedy; there is no other. Jesus is pursuing you, He cares for you, and His design for your marriage is that you would join together as one in the midst of the pain and be stronger together.

BRING IT HOME

- How would you describe your season of life? Individually? Together in your marriage?
- Pause for a moment and reflect on the fact that God sees you right now—in this very moment, despite what has happened and what is happening. How does it feel to be seen?
- What do you think Jesus sees when He looks at your marriage?

CELEBRATE THE SEASON

What calendar season are you in? Any holidays close to you? Sit down together and name your season according to where you are. Maybe it's the Summer of Adventures. Or the Fall of Recovery. Or the Winter of Mourning. Whether it's happy or sad, name your season, commemorate it, and decide what ceremonial action works for it. Maybe it's raising a glass, having a meal, summiting a mountain, or tossing something into a lake to float away. As you find what's beautiful in the season, discuss what it means to know you are looked at with love, right now, by the God who sees you both.

PRAYER

Father God, thank You for not only creating us (which is amazing) but for seeing us right now in the season we're in. We look to You and treasure Your promises. Thank You for sending Jesus to show us that we are seen by You in every single season. We love You. In Jesus' name, amen.

LOVE NOTES

The LORD God formed a man from the dust of the ground and breathed into his nostrils the breath of life, and the man became a living being.

GENESIS 2:7

CHAPTER 43

THE SIGNIFICANCE OF YOUR OTHER

JENNIE

while back, I was invited by a friend to a dinner party. The invitation said, "Your S/O is invited, also." I thought, *Okay, what is S/O?* I googled it and found out it means different things: special order, sold out, shout-out, sheriff's office, Shaquille O'Neal, system overload, shipping order . . . There were literally hundreds of things that S/O stood for, but what she meant was Significant Other. The party was BYOSO—bring your own significant other.

It made me laugh a little that I didn't know that, but then I got to thinking. God has been teaching me what it means to find the significance in your significant other. When we choose to see the significance in our significant others, and in ourselves, we will experience the purpose and the power God wants us to have.

Let's go back to the very beginning—that's always a good place to start. In Genesis 1–2 we see God creating and designing the world and all that is in it. As we've discussed in previous devotions, God is the Master Builder and delights in creating beautiful things. We get to read about His original design for the earth and for humans *and* for marriage. Genesis 2 specifically tells the story of how God made Adam from the dust of the ground and made Eve from Adam's rib (now *that's* thinking creatively).

It's so weird to me that God made man from dirt. I don't know why He did that, but I do know He is creative. God loves to make something out of nothing, and He does it like no one else. He made something significant from something insignificant. From dirt to two human beings. From nothing to something.

Incidentally, the elements that make up dirt are carbon, oxygen, nitrogen, phosphorous, sodium, iron, copper, and hydrogen. The elements that make up a human are very similar: oxygen, carbon, hydrogen, nitrogen, phosphorus, and calcium.[1] I look at dirt and feel amazed that God would even think, *Hey, I know! I should put some of this stuff together and make a human being, a complex creature made in My image.* It blows my mind and shows us that God created us—and that because of this, we have significance.

Next in the Genesis account, God made woman out of a man's rib. I think this is significant. For me, one of my favorite places to be is right next to Levi's side. And I love when we're in a crowd of people, and he comes up and just puts his arm around me, and I fit perfectly, right there, next to him. I belong there. Bible commentator Matthew Henry said, "[Eve] was not made out of his head to rule over him, nor out of his feet to be trampled by him, but out of his side to be equal with him. Under his arm to be protected, and near his heart to be loved."[2]

God designed us so beautifully. Who are you? You were specifically created by a God who loves you. You were expertly made, uniquely crafted, and there is no other person like you. You're the only you. But when God took some dirt and breathed into it, His breath is what made you special.

God's breath in you makes you significant. You become a work of art when God breathes in you. You become the masterpiece that God designed you to be. It's not surprising that most of the human body's mass is made up of oxygen—that's God's breath in us.[3] Our significance comes from the very breath of God.

Once you see the significance of the way you are created, you realize that God is still excited about the detail of who you are and who your spouse is—building you up, individually and together. And your job as a spouse is to stay curious about who you are and what God made you for—and how you and your spouse creatively complement each other.

We do need to fight to see the significance of our better halves sometimes. When it's hard to see, we've got to put on glasses like the one Spider-Man (Tom Holland) puts on in the movie *Spider-Man: Far from Home*. He puts on these glasses that Tony Stark made, and it shows him who each person is and weird facts about them. I think it's possible for you to put on a pair of rose-colored glasses and remind yourself of the significance of your spouse, best friend, confidant, lover—the one God made in His likeness and imbued with significance. Fight for it; you'll find it.

BRING IT HOME

- When you think of the Adam and Eve story, do you identify at all with God's means and materials of creation? Do you find it odd? Troubling? Amazing? Strangely truthful or accurate? How have you engaged with the story in the past?

- Do you believe that God is still building you and your mate with the same level of excitement and care He took in building Adam and Eve? How could you consider your marriage part of that "building"?

- Consider the significance of your other: How does God seem to be blending their gifts and strengths together with yours to make something even more beautiful? How is the Master Builder at work in you two?

WHEN WE CHOOSE TO SEE THE SIGNIFICANCE IN OUR SIGNIFICANT OTHERS, AND IN OURSELVES, WE WILL EXPERIENCE THE PURPOSE AND THE POWER GOD WANTS US TO HAVE.

FROM THE DIRT

Here's a fun idea: Grow something together. Plant a seed or a seedling in some dirt and put it in a window in your home to sprout. Or go to the garden center and pick out something already growing, or even a tree to plant in a special spot.

Get your hands into the dirt together, and bring something green and growing into your life to remind you that God is continually making something out of nothing, and that He breathed life and significance into your "other." As you watch the plant grow, remember that you can grow in purpose and power as you recognize your own significance and the significance of your "significant other."

PRAYER

Father God, You are so good. Thank You for breathing life into us so purposefully, not just on day six of creation but every single day. You give us significance. It's Your breath in our lungs, and we thank You for seeing strength and beauty in us, even when we don't see it. Help us see ourselves and each other with Your perspective and to walk in Your grace with each other. In Jesus' name, amen.

Do nothing from selfishness or empty conceit, but with humility consider one another as more important than yourselves.

PHILIPPIANS 2:3 NASB

CHAPTER 44

CHOOSE TO SEE THE GOOD

JENNIE

t's so important for us in our married relationships to *choose* to see the significance of our significant others. We actually have a choice in what we see. I think so many of us—me included—when we look at our spouses, at people, at the world around us, sometimes see only the negative. Because that's easy. I might walk into a room and immediately gauge how the space makes me feel—the flaws or imperfections or weirdly placed furniture. But instead of finding the flaws, I could work at finding something else.

I mentioned before that I have a note on my phone that's titled, "Being a Levi Aaron Lusko Expert." When he shows me something he loves, I put it in there. When he tells me something he's excited about, I put it in there. I try to observe, to watch, to figure out the things that make him tick and the things he loves, because I *want* to be a Levi Aaron Lusko expert. Now, imagine if I had a list on my phone of things that annoy me about Levi, and I consulted it regularly. The little imperfections. A record of mistakes. Wouldn't that completely change the tone of our lives? It would be ruinous. And I don't even want to think about it.

I encourage all of us who are married to be an expert on the *positive* things about your spouse. To choose to see the good. To choose to encourage. To choose to love. To choose to speak to the king, and not to the fool. We all have a king/queen in us and a fool. The one who is addressed is often the one who responds. And we get to choose who we look for in our spouses and help them become who they and we long for them to be. We can see the king/queen and speak life—lift them up and address that glorious person we fell for, not that fool only we get to see because we're in each other's business all the time. And on the other hand, it's amazing to be on the receiving end of this viewpoint, to know someone is choosing to see you as royalty when you *know* you've been hard to deal with. Nothing makes you feel so warm and secure. It's such a privilege that we get to do this for each other.

When today's verse says, "Consider one another as more important than yourselves," it is not about disregarding your own thoughts, hopes, and dreams. It is elevating the person in your life to honor them, think well of them, and lift them up. It's not diminishing you or tearing both them and yourself down. It's meekness. It's strength under control. It's being able to lift up someone else without pouring contempt on yourself or thinking of yourself as less-than.

Your spouse *is* significant. Choose to see it. And if you're having a hard time with that, ask God. He'll show you. Just look and see. If you need a jump start, try looking at yourself with true humility and asking, *What are my faults? What do I need to deal with? How does my spouse give me grace?* It's amazing how occupied you can become if you're examining your own faults and not theirs.

As you're growing together, you are learning more about yourself individually—all the good, the bad, and the ugly. And you're learning about your spouse. I love how Martin Luther called marriage "a school for character."[1] That is so true—*if* you choose to make it true. So, come on, let's do it!

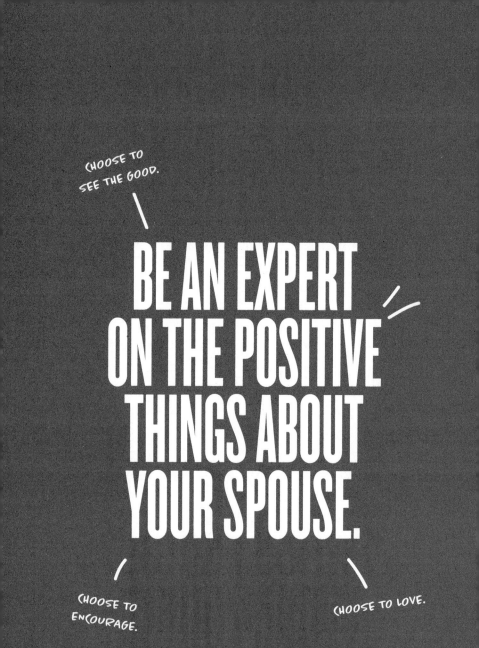

BRING IT HOME

- How can being an expert on your spouse—knowing the things they love and that make them tick—help you see the king/queen and not the fool?
- Have you asked God how He sees your spouse? What do you think He would say? How might His viewpoint and your viewpoint line up? How might yours be limited?
- How have you found marriage to be a school for character? What's been the hardest or best lesson?

BUILD YOUR EXPERT FILE

Okay, folks—it's time to become the expert. Open your Evernote or memo or get your pen and paper, and start your expert file on your spouse. List their full name at the top. Make your categories. Some might be:

- gifts
- movies/TV shows
- food/drinks
- music
- colors
- people
- clothing brands (add sizes too)
- break-time activities
- ways to blow off steam

The possibilities are as individual as your person. Do a mind dump of everything you know in those categories. Wherever it's looking scrappy, ask some probing questions. It's of course more fun to collect the data organically while seeing what delights them, but a little basic collection for your file couldn't hurt. Keep adding to it! You'll be glad you have it when you're looking for a way to serve, cheer up, or celebrate them.

PRAYER

Lord, thank You for bringing us together to be the number one supporters of each other and experts on each other. We are here for it. Give us eyes to see each other as truly significant and to be willing to sacrifice for each other in ways that move us forward together. In Jesus' name, amen.

Know therefore that the LORD your God is God; he is the faithful God, keeping his covenant of love to a thousand generations of those who love him and keep his commandments.

DEUTERONOMY 7:9

CHAPTER 45

THE GENERATIONS

JENNIE

Take a moment and think of the people in your life who make up your community. Chances are, these same people are the ones you hang out with, go on double dates with, and confide in when things are difficult. Do you have other couples in your life, or are you going it alone, trying to navigate life and its complexities on your own? It's good to have couple-friends who are similar to you, who are in the same age group and who get all your references and jokes. These friends know what you're going through in ways others don't. God bless these people. They are lifesavers. We definitely need them, and they need us.

What's important to be aware of, though, is that the community surrounding and supporting your marriage should also be varied. You should have friends of different ages, backgrounds, cultures—that's part of the guardrail system that can keep you from slipping off the road as a couple. There is a wealth of wisdom we can miss out on when we stay stuck in only our age group.

It makes me think of church—the best place to grow in Christ, meet your people, and let your roots go deep in a community through which God provides wisdom, strength, accountability, correction, conflict, abundant life, and fun. I love how the church is built of generations doing life together, learning together and from one another. Our church is full of people of every age, and it is beautiful to see. Every season of life is embraced and celebrated and honored. The old see the power of serving, leading, and being generous for the sake of reaching the next generation.

The young learn from older generations who have wisdom and knowledge gained from experience. There's power in leaning into the generations around us.

When it comes down to it, we're better together.

I don't see this too much these days, but I know some people live with grandparents in their home. I grew up with my Filipino grandfather and grandmother, Lolo and Lola, living with us when they weren't in the Philippines. And I'm so thankful for this. I remember washing the dishes and cooking with my Lola and learning so much from watching her. I've read that more and more families are choosing multigenerational housing arrangements, where a married couple will live with younger family members who don't have money to buy their own house, or with retired parents who need care.[1]

There's something beautiful about this multigenerational learning and sharing that can tend to get lost, but a healthy church can and should act like this as we grow in wisdom with those younger and older than us, as we do life together.

We need this in marriage too—desperately. We need to know what it looks like to be *happily* married. We need older, wiser couples to pour into our hearts and into our relationships. We need to also be living in a way that shows younger couples that it's possible to love each other through the heartache and difficult days.

God has given Levi and me all of the above, and we are so grateful. I encourage you to find these couples in your church and *be* these couples in your church. Maybe you'll want to talk with your pastor about stepping out in faith and starting a married-of-all-ages small group that meets and talks about the weekend's message along with the joys and struggles of life. It will be strengthening, deepening, empowering, and fun! You'll get to know the generations in your church.

The old with the young, the young with the old make all of us better. And the more we look at life the way God sees it, the less we're looking at what category we can place people into.

The Bible says that God thinks a lot about generations. Acts 2:39 says, "The promise is for you and your children and for all who are far off—for all whom the Lord our God will call." God looks past you today and sees your children, and He looks past your children and He sees your children's children, who today are far off. He looked past your grandparents and parents and saw you. But He sees them all as those He has called.

The Bible says God is faithful "to a thousand generations." Now, when we see the word *generation*, we're at a disadvantage because of our culture; we think Boomer, Millennial, Gen Z, and so on. We tend to put people in these rigid categories, but that's not how God sees them. He sees generations as all the people who are living on the earth at one time. He looks at us as those He has called, and He's faithful to a thousand generations looking forward.

The more we see God's heart, the more our eyes are opened to see people we can learn from and share with. There are people around us whom God wants to use in our lives and people whom God wants to bless through us. It's not about how old and how young they are, or how old or young we are, for that matter. Let's seek out the richness of generations and bring it into our relationships, and let's see God do the impossible in us and through us.

THE CHURCH IS BUILT UP OF
GENERATIONS DOING LIFE TOGETHER.

THERE'S A WEALTH OF WISDOM WE CAN MISS OUT ON WHEN WE STAY STUCK IN ONLY OUR AGE GROUP.

YOU SHOULD HAVE FRIENDS OF
DIFFERENT AGES, BACKGROUNDS, AND CULTURES.

BRING IT HOME

- Do you tend to feel an affinity for people in a certain generation over another? Or a disconnect? Why is that?
- What does it change to consider that God sees all people on earth as one generation?
- Consider the mix of older and younger people you spend time with as a couple. How can you work on having a more varied and diverse community? Who could you pursue?

CONVERSATION STARTERS

- "One thing I've learned about marriage and relationships from someone in an older generation is _____."
- "Something I've learned about relationships from someone in a younger generation is _____."
- "One way we might find some older and younger generational diversity in our mix is _____."

PRAYER

Lord God, thank You for being a multigenerational, multicultural, multicreative God. The way You delight in using anyone who is willing to serve You is mind-blowing. We want to grow in learning from a variety of individuals and couples. We surrender to how You are weaving us into this beautiful design You are continuing to create. Let the richness of Your love and creativity overwhelm us and open our eyes to see what You are already doing around us, and give us the vision and wisdom to enter in and engage. This is going to be fun! We love You, Lord. In Jesus' name, amen.

PART 11

UNLEASH THE BLESSINGS

LOVE NOTES

Isaac sowed in that land, and reaped in the same year a hundredfold; and the Lord blessed him. The man began to prosper, and continued prospering until he became very prosperous.

GENESIS 26:12–13 NKJV

CHAPTER 46

AIN'T NO FOUNTAIN HIGH ENOUGH

LEVI AND JENNIE

oday's verses are more relatable than you might think. While you may not consider yourself in a season of prospering—maybe things are pretty tough right now—the prospering in these verses are sandwiched between some real drama. (Perhaps some drama that's a bit like your own.) In our marriage, we have found that times of prosperity and growth tend to be snuck right into hard moments, times of failure, heartache, and the mess of life. Which is comforting, because *that* is real life—even if we'd rather not admit it.

Like we studied earlier, Genesis 24 gives us the beautiful love story of Isaac and Rebekah—a big high in their lives. In Genesis 25 we see the intense and turbulent pregnancy and birth of the twins, Esau and Jacob, along with a super dramatic struggle over Esau's birthright.

In Genesis 26 we find Isaac and Rebekah in the middle of a famine, but the Lord promised to bless and take care of Isaac and his descendants. But right after this moment of God speaking to Isaac, some men in the land of Gerar asked Isaac about Rebekah, and he told them that she was his sister (v. 7). *Red alert. Red alert.*

Isaac was caught in his lie. And why did he lie to the king of the Philistines? Fear for his life. What? Isaac? Really? The God of the universe had just promised him (just as He'd promised his father, Abraham) that He would be with him and bless him and make his descendants multiply as the stars of heaven. What was Isaac thinking?

But this isn't too far from us, right? How often do we hear from God and experience His love and power, but then go on in our own power and operate out of fear? This can be one of the greatest struggles in life. God does a beautiful work in us, our lives are changed and transformed, and in a moment, in a flash, we make a mess. Bless our hearts.

But thank God that His love for us and desire to dwell with us aren't based on us and our magnificent ability to make a royal mess of our lives!

The very next verses say that "Isaac sowed in that land, and reaped in the same year a hundredfold; and the LORD blessed him. The man began to prosper, and continued prospering until he became very prosperous" (vv. 12–13 NKJV). What a juxtaposition. God brought them out of a hot mess and triple prospered Isaac and Rebekah.

It's possible to experience growth and increase even in the midst of our faults and failures in marriage. We lay this out here to give you hope.

But here's the thing: Isaac had to take care of some dirty work in the fields before he could reap bountifully. He had to dig.

The book of Genesis goes on to tell us that the Philistines had filled Isaac's wells with earth after Abraham died. The Philistines had envied Abraham, and they also envied Isaac, so they went out of their way to try to prevent Isaac from prospering.

To have these flocks, crops, and herds, Isaac needed water to sustain them. The water had to come from wells, but the only way Isaac could get this water was to dig out the dirt from the wells that had been dug before. It was a common tactic in that day to put rocks in someone's field, to cut down trees, and to stop up wells so they would have nowhere to get water. And sometimes that was a death sentence.

What was Isaac's response to seeing wells that weren't flowing? To dig out the dirt that was clogging them. In this, we have a picture of what it takes to unblock the flow of God's blessing in marriage. Because God intends for marriage to be a source of life—a fountain.

We saw in an earlier entry that Solomon described marriage as a fountain: "Let your fountain be blessed, and rejoice with the wife of your youth" (Proverbs 5:18 NKJV). Your marriage is meant to be a fountain—spouting high and far, bringing hydration, strength, joy, and peace everywhere you go. Come on, sing it with us: *"Ain't no fountain high enough . . ."*

Our marriages are supposed to point people to the ultimate marriage—what it looks like to have a relationship with God (Ephesians 5:21–33). We are meant to point to the Living Water, Jesus, who can quench the thirst of a weary and dissatisfied humanity. Unfortunately, our marriages, which are designed to flow with fresh water, tend to get blocked with the very thing that makes up who we are physically—dirt. Ironically, we can be the ones who stop up the flow, whether it's pain or sin from our past or an attitude that is rude and lacks gratitude.

But the good news? God invites us to be a part of the answer to unleashing the fresh flow of blessing within marriage.

It takes a willingness to daily dig out the dirt that the Enemy wants to scoop into our wells. Dirt happens. No need to be ashamed. But remember that your marriage is full of potential sources of hydration to a thirsty world, and to you too. And God actively wants to bless you.

GOD INTENDS FOR
MARRIAGE TO BE
A SOURCE OF LIFE.

We believe with all our hearts that God wants to prosper you and bless you and use you. He wants to bless your family, your marriage, and your kids. James 1:16–18 in *The Message* says, "So, my very dear friends, don't get thrown off course. Every desirable and beneficial gift comes out of heaven. The gifts are rivers of light cascading down from the Father of Light. There is nothing deceitful in God, nothing two-faced, nothing fickle. He brought us to life using the true Word, showing us off as the crown of all his creatures."

The Father of Light wants *rivers of light* to cascade from your life and from your marriage. Now *that's* a fountain.

So how do you start to address the clogged wells in your marriage? Remind each other of the purpose God has for you together. This is important because we have short memories. We need reminders every day, and we need to fight to remember who we are and whose we are. We need to pull an Isaac and dig out the wells—the different aspects of what it takes to walk in relationship, to walk in marriage, to thrive and fight, to flourish together—even in the midst of our shortcomings and mistakes and mess-ups. Our God is good. And in His goodness, He is more than able to make rivers of water flow out of something that was once dry and dead and stopped up. Let it be so in our hearts and in our lives and in our marriages.

BRING IT HOME

- Do you truly believe that God actively wants to bless you? Is there any area of your life or marriage where you have just assumed you're not blessed and given up hope?

- If you have resigned yourself to a dry and withered area that lacks in blessing, prosperity, hope, and goodness, why is that? What convinced you that you're not meant to be blessed this way?
- What kind of dirt is the devil trying to throw on you? What would happen if you started digging in this area?

CONVERSATION STARTERS

- "When I think about other people being blessed by our marriage, I feel _____. How is this a realistic possibility for us?"
- "One blessing that we currently enjoy that could bring life to others is _____. How could we expand there?"
- "What if the very places we feel the most hopeless are the ones where God wants to bring blessing? What would those blessings look like?"

PRAYER

Creator God, You are willing to dig deep into our hearts, to search us and know us and find the things within us that You want to cleanse away and also make new. Thank You that as we put ourselves in Your hands, You are more than able to do the impossible in our hearts and lives. We surrender to You, and we are willing to dig out the things that have been clogging our wells. We submit to Your plan for our marriage to be a fountain that flows freely, ferociously, and far. There is nothing hidden from You, and nothing Your love and power can't touch and change in our relationship. Thank You, Lord. In Jesus' name, amen.

LOVE NOTES

Be sure you know the condition of your flocks,
give careful attention to your herds.

PROVERBS 27:23

CHAPTER 47

YOUR WELLNESS CHECK

LEVI AND JENNIE

The yearly doctor's visits for checkups are dreaded in the Lusko home. Our kids fight it, even if there is a promised trip to the local ice cream shop immediately afterward. It's the shots; it's the waiting; it's the being in a stuffy office. Every well check for the kids includes a dramatized parental monologue describing the life-saving benefits of doctor visits and how they need them for their continued health. We also try to explain how important it is for the doctor to check on their growth and overall strength of their bodies and minds. And adult well checks aren't much better! The older we get, the more invasive the checkups become, poking and prodding and examining. But we know to endure it because it's for our health and longevity.

Just like checkups for our bodies are important for health, so it is with the things God has given us. Our verse today tells us to know the state of our flocks and herds (Proverbs 27:23). I like how *The Message* says it: "Know your sheep by name; carefully attend to your flocks." It continues to explain,

> (Don't take them for granted;
>> possessions don't last forever, you know.)
> And then, when the crops are in
>> and the harvest is stored in the barns,
> You can knit sweaters from lambs' wool,
>> and sell your goats for a profit;
> There will be plenty of milk and meat
>> to last your family through the winter. (vv. 24–27)

On a practical level these verses remind us of how important it is to take extra care of our resources and sources of income, because wisdom warns us that riches don't last forever. We don't know what crashes in the market or natural disaster or emergency will happen, but we can plan and prepare and take care of what God has given us.

Just as there is wisdom in taking care of our jobs and resources, there is also great wisdom in taking care of the relationships God has given us. In your marriage a good question to ask is, "So . . . how are we doing?" and then to sit and listen to your spouse's response.

In our marriage one of us is generally more optimistic and tends to see life through rose-colored glasses (Levi), and the other tends to see the negative first as a preventative measure (Jennie—I'm trying to learn and grow, guys!). In all of our marriages we can really only be as strong as the weakest part, so it's important, regardless of the rose- or gray-colored glasses we tend to look through, to speak up about how we're doing and how we think we're doing together.

This is for all of us, to take notes on our marriages, like a yearly checkup. And what's so amazing is, as you're regularly checking up on your relationship, you can find out, "Okay, are we dipping down below where we should be? Or are we aiming higher than we should be, too far above the target?"

Let's not forget, as we're checking in on our marriages, that we're all in different places. We're all on different journeys in our walks with the Lord and in our marriages. Some of us are more mature than others, and we just need to, in this moment, receive what God has for us in our different wells. Some of us have some big digging to do. It's going to be different every day for every couple.

But it's good and healthy to ask, "How's our marriage? Is it a fountain or a dried-up well?" It can be a complicated answer, and that's okay. It can be good here, bad there, great in one area, not so great in another. One well is flowing, and another well is blocked. So you spend a week digging it out. Meanwhile other wells are filling up with dirt as you're working on the first one. You can see it as discouraging, or you can see it as part of the process of the hard work to keep your relationship vibrant.

And marriage is always about diligence. The New King James Version of today's verse puts it this way: "Be diligent to know the state of your flocks, and attend to your herds." Our responsibility is to be diligent *and* to attend. Working hard and caring for. Repeat. Our marriages are living things, dynamic and changing, constantly growing. There's a pulse to them. There's a vibe to health. So we keep asking and digging and giving and hoping and respecting and loving, and doing it again the next day, and then the next. And then we look back and see God's faithfulness and the work He was doing in us all along.

It's like the process of painting the Golden Gate Bridge. The moment they finish, they go back to the beginning and have to start again because the front end is already faded and rusted. What a helpful picture as we consider the care and keeping of our marriages too. Our relationships are always in flux. They are always in progress. As we keep up with the habit of painting, maintaining, checking, connecting, and being aware, the result will be a fresh, flourishing, and fun relationship.

BRING IT HOME

- How can the fact that there is always work to be done in marriage, always something that's not in good shape, and always

JUST AS THERE IS WISDOM IN TAKING CARE OF OUR JOBS AND RESOURCES, THERE IS ALSO GREAT WISDOM IN TAKING CARE OF THE RELATIONSHIPS GOD HAS GIVEN US.

KEEP ASKING AND DIGGING AND GIVING AND HOPING AND RESPECTING AND LOVING, AND DOING IT AGAIN THE NEXT DAY, AND THEN THE NEXT DAY.

some maintenance needed, actually free you from guilt in your walk toward a healthier marriage? Does it help to understand that problems are par for the course?

- Are you in the habit of checking the health of your relationship? How do you do it? What might be an impediment to that practice? How can you clear it?
- Over the past few months, how would you describe the pulse or health vibe of your relationship? What have been the ups and downs? How have your needs fluctuated from day to day, week to week?

MAKE AN APPOINTMENT

- Just as we schedule a yearly physical, sit down and brainstorm what a yearly wellness check for your marriage would look like.
- Would you go away for a weekend? Rent a cabin? How would you protect your time and nurture yourselves?
- How would you make it fun and cozy?
- What items would you bring to the discussion?
- What kinds of indicators would let you know if you are within your target range for health?
- Check some dates on your calendar, do some research for a getaway or a staycation, and schedule your checkup retreat—maybe for a time after you conclude this devotional. Even once a year, a checkup can stave off decline and keep you on the path to health.

PRAYER

Lord God, You have given us our relationship, and we declare to You and to each other that we want to grow in diligence and in the care and keeping of it. We know it takes hard work, and where we are weak, we recognize that You are strong, so be our strength and be our joy. Thank You that when we are diligent with and aware of what You have given us that we can not only say, "It is well with my soul," but also say, "It is well with our marriage." In Jesus' name, amen.

LOVE NOTES

Thanks be to God who always leads us in triumph in Christ, and through us diffuses the fragrance of His knowledge in every place. For we are to God the fragrance of Christ among those who are being saved and among those who are perishing.

2 CORINTHIANS 2:14–15 NKJV

CHAPTER 48

SMELL MY VICTORY

LEVI AND JENNIE

W hether or not we like to admit it out loud, we all want to be victorious in our lives, to live triumphantly and powerfully, beautifully and fully. We don't set out at the start of our careers and declare to the world, "I want to be just okay at this job. I don't want to stand out and be brave to forge new paths. I just want to be mediocre and not attempt anything great!"

It's the same in our parenting. We don't sit at dinner with friends when we're expecting our first child and explain to them, "We really just want to barely parent our child. We want to barely feed and train him and then let him figure out everything on his own. We don't want to be awesome parents. Just average will do."

And yes, you guessed it, it's the same for our marriages too. We don't go on a walk with one of our favorite married couples and announce, "We really just want to skate through marriage and make the least impact on the world. We don't want to be an example to other couples; we are happy to have a weak and insignificant relationship."

Nope. It's the opposite, right? We start out with high hopes and dreams. We think about all the what-ifs and now-whats and if-only-we-coulds. We aspire to be great at what we do and how we approach this thing called living.

If this is so, why can there be such a distance between our dreams of what our marriages could be and what they are in real time? Is it even possible for our marriages to keep going and end as good as or even better than it started?

We are here to tell you the good news: *Yes!* It's possible to have a vibrant, victorious relationship. The news you may not want to hear? It takes *work*. Daily work.

It takes walking triumphantly in Christ every single day.

Maybe you're saying, "Levi, Jennie, what does that even mean?" We're so glad you asked.

In today's verses, Paul was in the middle of his letter to the church in Corinth. That church was a mixed bunch of people from all walks of life. While this gave it beautiful diversity and liveliness, it also sometimes caused division. Some splintering. The congregation needed a fresh infusion of leadership. In these chapters we can hear in his tone the love Paul had for this church and the people within it. Although Paul had to say some tough things, you can feel the love in his heart and the hope he had for this church to live brilliantly, extraordinarily, and victoriously.

He said in verse 14, "Now thanks be to God." This is a great place to start. Gratitude greases the wheels of our relationships. If we're desiring to live greatly, we need to start with thanks to our God, our Creator, our Savior, our Friend. The church has endless things to be grateful for, but Paul continued and said we should specifically thank Him because He "always leads us in triumph in Christ."

He always leads us. As children of God, we have the privilege of having the Creator of the universe be our Shepherd and the One who leads us.

Are you in need of wisdom? He leads you.

Are you in need of strength? He leads you.

No idea what your next step is? He leads you.

Say this psalm out loud:

The LORD is my shepherd;
I shall not want.
He makes me to lie down in green pastures;
He leads me beside the still waters.
He restores my soul;
He leads me in the paths of righteousness
For His name's sake.

Yea, though I walk through the valley of the shadow
of death,
I will fear no evil;
For You are with me;
Your rod and Your staff, they comfort me.

You prepare a table before me in the presence of my
enemies;
You anoint my head with oil;
My cup runs over.
Surely goodness and mercy shall follow me
All the days of my life;
And I will dwell in the house of the LORD
Forever. (Psalm 23 NKJV)

Years ago we challenged our church to memorize this psalm together. It was so special to memorize it as a church and to recite it as a family. (And goodness, it's getting harder and harder to memorize verses as we get older!) Memorizing this psalm has changed our lives. We say it with the kids at night sometimes. We say it when we're afraid and when we don't know what to do. And it

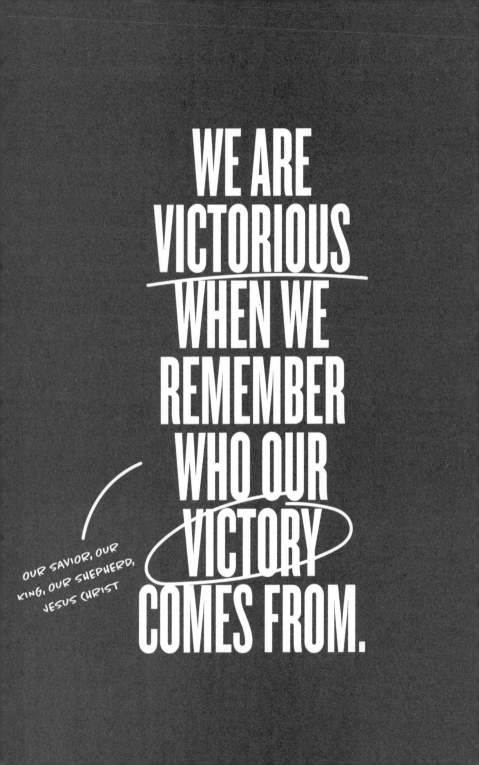

truly comforts us. Not because it's a religious thing that we learned one time. It's comforting because it reminds us who our Shepherd is. It reminds us of who is in control. It reminds us that God knows us, holds us, prepares us, and leads us. There's nothing more comforting than knowing that the Creator of the universe is our Shepherd. That's true confidence.

God leads us in triumph *in Christ.* This phrase comes up almost a hundred times in the Bible, and it is the key ingredient to our lives. Triumphant living comes when—and only when—we are in Christ. Our marriages will only be as strong as we are individually in Christ, together making Him the center. We are victorious when we remember who our victory comes from: our Savior, our King, our Shepherd, Jesus Christ.

Just in case you missed it, *Jesus* is the answer to the ache within. We were separated from God because of our sin, but God had the remedy. His name is Jesus. He came at Christmas, was born of a virgin, lived a perfect life, died a sinless death, and defeated the grave by rising from the dead. This is where our victory comes from!

When we remember this, we can truly live out what comes next in these verses in 2 Corinthians: Christ, who "through us diffuses the fragrance of His knowledge in every place" (NKJV). Did you catch that? We are meant to diffuse the fragrance of His knowledge in every place. Well, that sounds lovely, but what does it mean? We might think of an essential oil diffuser, but it's more powerful than that. We see in the next verse that "we are to God the fragrance of Christ among those who are being saved and among those who are perishing" (NKJV).

First and foremost, God smells this fragrance. Our lives are meant to be glorifying to God first, and that's a choice we can only make for ourselves. We can't make it for our spouses, and our spouses can't make it for us. No one can walk with Jesus for us. No one can be the fragrance of Christ for us. But as we allow the fragrance of Christ to permeate our hearts, souls, and minds, we will diffuse His knowledge in every place.

And when something is diffused, it fills a room. It's like the scene of Mary pouring out the costly oil on Jesus' feet right before His death and burial (Matthew 26:6–13; Mark 14:3–9). If she poured out the whole alabaster flask of this costly oil, we know that fragrance filled the entire room.

And that is how God designed us: to fill a room with the fragrance of Christ. Not in an overbearing "too much pumpkin spice candle" smell in a small living room. We are meant to beautifully and vibrantly fill every place with the fragrance of Christ. As we live it out in our own hearts and lives, the next place it should fill is our marriages. We let the fragrance of Christ fill our marriages, and then it can truly be the picture of Christ and the church that it is meant to be.

Imperfectly? Yes. But victoriously? Also yes.

BRING IT HOME

- What kinds of things are you most dreaming of being victorious in right now? As individuals? As a couple?
- If that victory comes from the leadership of Christ—exactly in

WE ARE MEANT TO BEAUTIFULLY AND VIBRANTLY FILL EVERY PLACE WITH THE FRAGRANCE OF CHRIST.

those areas—how can you start seeking that leadership and relying on Him more?

- Have you ever been in the presence of someone who was filling the room with an amazing spiritual fragrance? What was that experience like? Why do you think they were that way?

THE LORD IS YOUR SHEPHERD

You guessed it: we're going to ask you to memorize Psalm 23. Even if you've memorized it in the past, or if it's been a while, we encourage you to dive into it in a new way.

There are six verses, so maybe you'll want to take one a day this week. Speak them to each other. Write them on notes and stick them around the house. You could try writing them out, repeating them as you exercise or on your commute, and praying them together. At the end of each day, reflect on what each nugget means for you—individually and as a couple—as your Shepherd leads you toward victory.

PRAYER

Lord God, thank You for the victory You have given us in Christ Jesus! Thank You for making a way for us when there was no way on our own. Thank You for being our Shepherd and the One who not only leads us but who loves to lead us. Help us in our relationship to continue to make You the center of our hearts individually and then together. Remind us of the design You gave marriage to be a picture of Your love for Your people. We choose to walk triumphantly in Christ and to be the fragrance of Christ to You and to all the people in our lives. We love You. In Jesus' name, amen.

LOVE NOTES

A time to weep and a time to laugh,
a time to mourn and a time to dance.

ECCLESIASTES 3:4

CHAPTER 49

YOUR FAVORITE PART

LEVI AND JENNIE

We wish we could sit down together with you in real life. We wish we could get together at your local spot, sit in a quad of comfy chairs, and have coffee together. We could talk about life and love and marriage and ask you, "What's your favorite part?"

You'd probably make us smile or crack us up or make us snort coffee through our noses (vanilla oat-milk latte for Jennie and Americano for Levi), and we'd all have a moment together just thinking about how lucky we are. In all this talk of the times we've slipped and skidded and ended up in a big marital heap on the ground, it's worth it to take a moment and remember our favorite parts.

So think of this as a chance to have coffee together. Or tea. Or whatever. To talk a little bit about relationships. Sound good?

All right. We'll start off.

What is our favorite part of marriage?

JENNIE

Honestly, it's fun. I mean, Levi, you're my best friend. And I love doing life with you. I think my favorite thing is the little moments, like at dinner with the kids when I look up and see you there and think, *We're a family.* I love being a parent with you. I love being a mom and dad together. I love being married to you. I love our weird humor and inside jokes. It's ridiculous.

We're going to be celebrating twenty years before too long, and I am still growing more in love with you. And I love the little jokes that maybe we thought were long gone but just keep coming through our marriage.

In the hard parts, I love how you take care of me. I feel so safe. I like to say that my favorite spot is right next to you, and that's the truth. I even love growing old and wrinkly together.

It's just *fun*—I can't describe it any other way. What would you say?

LEVI

I would say obviously the big things are great, but I appreciate the random little ones. Sitting in front of the fire together. Driving in the car and not needing to say anything. Making you laugh by doing some silly little dance when I catch your eye while you're doing something important. It all adds up to something great as a whole. Honestly, before we were married, everyone told me how hard marriage was. No one told me how fun it is. I almost went into marriage stressed out because I didn't want to fail. I was thinking, *Oh my gosh, it's going to be so hard.* Because everyone likes to talk about the nitty-gritty part. You ask, "How's marriage?" And they go, "Oh, it's tough. It's a struggle. You need prayer."

Yikes.

So I went in expecting it to be a mess. And obviously, marriage is hard at times. Conflict is unavoidable. We go through difficulties. We get mad. But then there's makeup sex. So maybe that's my favorite part.

JENNIE

So true. While makeup sex *is* awesome, the regular kind is pretty incredible. Heart eyes emoji.

LEVI

All right. But the fun moments are like you say—little. I still like brushing our teeth together. Especially with our new toothbrushes. (How dorky are we? We are so obsessed with our cool electric toothbrushes that stick on the mirror. If Batman had a toothbrush, it would be this toothbrush.)

I remember we used to always brush our teeth together on the phone when we were engaged and dating.

Saying things like, "No, you hang up."

"No, no, *you* hang up."

We'd fall asleep on the phone together, remember?

So the first time after we were married, we were brushing our teeth, eyeballing each other like, "Well, hello there, hot stuff." It was amazing to be together in that moment and see what you looked like brushing your teeth. I haven't gotten over that. Never will.

So I would say my favorite part is all the moments. All the in-between ones, all the fun ones. Grieving, laughing, camping, from our earliest date nights at Costco to, hopefully, getting to do something really special for our twentieth. I love them all.

That's what we'd say to you. And we'd ask you to take a turn telling us what your favorite part is. Because it's serious business, going through this slippery-when-wet process, or navigating

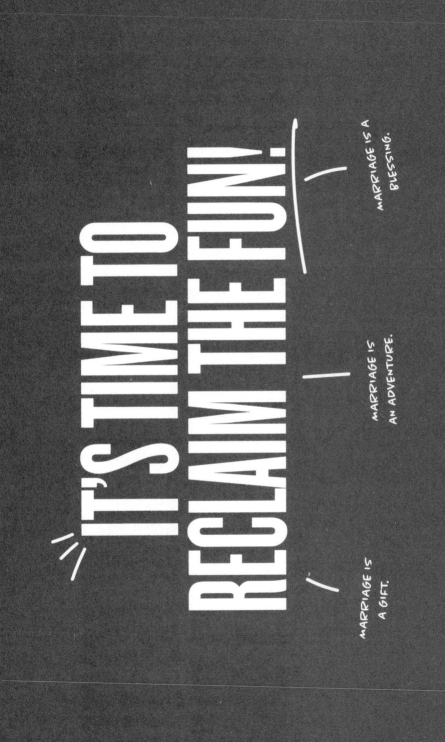

through the unstable parts of life with caution. It's so important to stop and remember: *Marriage is an adventure.* It's a gift. It's a blessing. It's time to reclaim the fun! It's yours, and it's so individual to you. We don't ever want to forget this stuff, because that's what our lives are built out of. Little moments like this.

So what about you? We're leaning forward, mugs warming our hands, listening.

BRING IT HOME

- Thinking back through your marriage and when you were dating, what is the most fun you've had in every part? From big moments to little moments, when have you had a great time together? You can go back and separate the time into segments, years, or seasons if that helps.
- Did anyone ever tell you how hard marriage was? Did anyone tell you how fun it was? What about your perception of marriage going in has changed over time?
- What would you say are your top inside jokes? How does your person make you laugh?

COFFEE TALK

Consider inviting a trusted friend couple out for coffee— preferably a pair that seems to have a good time together. Swap some stories. Have a laugh. In the course of your conversation, store up some good times in your memory, and draw from one another's experiences to find good ideas to keep the fun going in the future.

If it's awkward to ask them out on a couple date, try something like, "Hey! We noticed that you guys seem to have such a good time together, and we kind of want to hear some stories about you two and how you met and how you got to be so fun. It'd be great to spend some time with you."

PRAYER

God, thank You for this gift of marriage. Thank You for giving us a safe and sacred space to be ourselves, have fun, be weird, and enjoy life. Help us to remember and savor our favorite parts. Marriage is so good, and we want to count the ways. In Jesus' name, amen.

PART 12

FINDING THE WAY FORWARD

LOVE NOTES

In their hearts humans plan their course,
but the Lᴏʀᴅ establishes their steps.

PROVERBS 16:9

CHAPTER 50

YOU IN FIVE YEARS

JENNIE

Here's a good and healthy question to ask ourselves every now and then: Who do you want to be in five years? On your own? As a couple? As a family? It's a great mental and soulful exercise to make ourselves think ahead and consider who we want to be. And to reflect on how we're living now—in both the big and little things—will impact who we are in the future.

Living carefully and intentionally now will directly impact our future. This is wisdom. In Ephesians 5:15–16 Paul said, "See that you walk carefully [living life with honor, purpose, and courage; shunning those who tolerate and enable evil], not as the unwise, but as wise [sensible, intelligent, discerning people], making the very most of your time [on earth, recognizing and taking advantage of each opportunity and using it with wisdom and diligence], because the days are [filled with] evil" (AMP).

We can protect our future and our relationships by living carefully right now. As much as considering the future is helpful to present-day living, it's also important to consider what we're going through now as training for the trial we're not yet in. Because we can always imagine ourselves in five years—who we will be, what our marriages will be like, and what our lives will look like—but sometimes life turns out differently than how we thought it would.

For our family, almost ten years ago, we were in the depths of grief and loss. Our five-year-old daughter, Lenya, had an asthma attack and died suddenly, leaving us for heaven without notice or warning. In the five years of Lenya's life, we didn't think her birth was a countdown to her death only five years later. That was a trial we had no idea how to train for.

So that's why I tell you, from the deepest part of my heart, that we should be asking ourselves how we are training for the trial we are not yet in. Who will we be when tragedy hits our homes and our lives? How will we trust God in the midst of disappointment and pain and heartache?

When everything we thought our lives would be is taken away, what can't be taken away is Jesus. As we live a life of clinging to Him and trusting Him, we are preparing for when life shifts and it hits the fan.

We mentioned Katherine and Jay Wolf earlier.

Katherine experienced a stroke that came out of nowhere, and it drastically changed their lives. She wrote of her time in therapy after the stroke, "None of us asked to be there, and none of us could change the fact that we were there. As hot water and tears streamed down my face, I resolved to work my hardest in therapy, so I could get out of there as soon as possible. I also decided not to let my circumstances make me bitter or hopeless. I wanted to be able to encourage and inspire this new community."[1]

Before her stroke, Katherine was a model and was exploring an acting career. If you had talked with her before, she might have said something like, "In five years I'll probably be in a movie. In five years I'll probably be a model for this brand." She had her whole life ahead of her.

And then this stroke totally blindsided them and changed life as they knew it, to where Katherine was using a wheelchair for mobility and has had major health issues. But both Katherine and Jay have held on to Jesus. The things they learned in the sunshine

LIFE TENDS NOT TO GO AS PLANNED, AND IN THOSE MOMENTS, WE HAVE A CHOICE TO TRUST GOD.

WE CAN MAKE THE DECISION TO TRAIN FOR THE TRIAL WE'RE NOT YET IN.

of life, they have lived in the shade. Both she and Jay had spent time focusing on Jesus and on the things that couldn't be taken away, and that sustained them when the storm hit and sent their lives careening off the track they had laid for themselves. We are so thankful for the way they shine so bright.

Life tends not to go as planned, and in those moments, we have a choice to trust God. But also in the days leading up to the unknown trials, we have a choice to live in a way that will set us up for strength and success—living wisely, walking carefully.

As our verse today says, we can plan our ways, but God is the one who directs our steps. We have to give Him the space and the runway to move in our lives—when we feel great *and* when we feel horrible. When life goes along with our five-year plan *and* when it doesn't. We can make that decision to train for the trial that we're not yet in. We can do anything when we run to Jesus in the sunshine *and* in the shade.

You in five years? No matter what is to come for you and for your marriage, you can be stronger, kinder, humbler, more joyful, and more gracious as you train now for what is to come.

And if your vows are tested,

> for better, for worse,
> for richer, for poorer,
> in sickness and in health,
> to love and to cherish,
> till death do us part,

then God wants to remind you that He's your Father and He loves you. You're not alone in the test. But the test, the trial, is there for a purpose far greater than you can fully know. Let the apostle James remind you and encourage you:

> My brethren, count it all joy when you fall into various trials, knowing that the testing of your faith produces patience. But let patience have its perfect work, that you may be perfect and complete, lacking nothing. If any of you lacks wisdom, let him ask of God, who gives to all liberally and without reproach, and it will be given to him. (James 1:2–5 NKJV)

Friends, there is far more at work here than you can even see. Let the test do its work in you. Let the trial do its work in your marriage. Allow God to direct your heart and your steps, and watch Him do impossible and beautiful things that will stun you. You will be filled with wonder at who He is and with anticipation for what He will continue to do.

BRING IT HOME

- When you worry that the worst will happen, what do you worry about?
- What would it look like to run to Jesus in that situation?
- How does knowing we can rely on Jesus give us strength to hope and plan for the future, even if it is uncertain?

CONVERSATION STARTERS

- "For me, something that has gone completely contrary to the plans I made in the past is _____."

NO MATTER WHAT WHAT IS TO COME FOR YOU AND FOR YOUR MARRIAGE, YOU CAN BE BE STRONGER, KINDER, HUMBLER, MORE JOYFUL, AND MORE GRACIOUS AS YOU TRAIN NOW FOR WHAT IS IS TO COME.

WE CAN DO EVERYTHING WHEN WE RUN TO JESUS IN THE SUNSHINE AND THE SHADE.

- "One way I'd like to strengthen and prioritize my relationship with Jesus is _____."
- "I have hope for our future, no matter what happens, because _____."

PRAYER

Father God, You are the Good Shepherd and the Master Planner and Director. You allow things to happen in our lives not to harm us but to cause us to run to You and to do the deep work in our souls and hearts and minds that only You can do. So we tell You, and each other, that we trust You. When You test us, we want to seek You more and prefer each other more. We want to walk through the trial with the confidence, strength, and power that come only from You, our perfect Father. Thank You that You are the One who can take broken, hurting, weak people and transform us into Your whole, healed, strong children who give You all the glory and all the praise. We surrender. In Jesus' name, amen.

The silver-haired head is a crown of glory,
if it is found in the way of righteousness.

PROVERBS 16:31 NKJV

CHAPTER 51

I WANNA GROW OLD WITH YOU

JENNIE

A study was done a while back in which people in America were asked, "Would you want to live to be one hundred?" Such a great question. If you can believe it, more than 40 percent said no. More than a third said, "I do not want to live to be one hundred years old."[1] This means two out of five people in America would rather be dead than old. It seems to me this is a consensus that there's little to no value in old age.

I understand that there are complications with old age, especially into the one hundred range. I get that when the elderly (and their families) struggle through Alzheimer's or memory loss or their overall health declining, it's painful. It's hard to see the effects of aging on the people we love.

I guess if I had to answer this question honestly, I might choose death over living to one hundred, because I'm pretty sure I will be a crazy old great-grandma. I don't want to speak this over myself, but I already struggle with memory. I'd rather be in heaven with Jesus and *not* be a burden to my kids and their kids. *Mom! She's doing it again! Grandma is walking around in her robe, chasing down the mailman, waving her slice of pizza in the air, and angry about the rum being gone!*

As much as it makes me laugh to think about Alivia, Daisy, Clover, and Lennox dealing with me being really old, it *is* a sobering question.

The thing is, old age doesn't have to be dreadful or frightening. It can be celebrated and admired and maybe even looked forward to. It's possible to love the golden years, holding tight to and pouring out golden wisdom, and to find beauty in the golden years of marriage too.

Our culture seems to idolize youth. I mean, I get it—in our youth we have energy and tight, glowing skin, no saggy parts, and there's an innocence and hope and excitement about the future. As we age, so many of us try to avoid gray hair and wrinkles, but there is something about a happy, wise, gray-haired person that is comforting.

(Side note: An angry, unwise, gray-haired person is not as comforting, and that's a reminder that how we live *now* will be how we are *then*. If we spend our lives frowning and being angry, we will have angry wrinkles on our faces and in our hearts. I think if we spend our lives smiling and with joy, we will wear beautiful wrinkles and shine out beautiful hearts.)

My daughter Daisy and I were walking out of Target recently (with only one bag! Celebrate the tiny wins, people!) when we saw this stunning older woman who had long, beautiful silver hair. Daisy and I looked at each other, and I whispered, "Wow, she's gorgeous! I want to have long, silver hair like that when I'm older." And Daisy whispered back (at age eleven), "Me too!"

Proverbs 16:31 gives us a precious perspective on old age. "The silver-haired head is a crown of glory, *if* it is found in the way of righteousness" (NKJV). Now that's a big *if*. (This, by the way, is why when I try to grab the one gray hair Levi has on his beard, he won't let me. He's like, "No, no—don't. I earned this.")

How have you two imagined growing old together, a silver crown of glory on both your heads? What are your dreams? Your plans? Your fears? No matter what age you are now, I'm betting you have a vision in your minds of what things are going to be like for you in your final years. That crown of glory can be yours.

What this verse doesn't say is that old is automatically wise. The key phrase is "if it is found in the way of righteousness." The truth is, you can be young and wicked, and you can be old and foolish. So the key is what is in your heart—what God is doing in your soul. Righteous young people can become righteous old people. Wicked young people can become wicked old people. The passing of time can either wear and break you down as a couple, or it can season you and strengthen you. Today, no matter your age, you can choose which direction you're going together.

It's vital that we hold on to wisdom. The book of Proverbs has thirty-one chapters in it, and speaking from experience, I can say that it will help you learn and grow in wisdom. I love reading a proverb every day, no matter where else I am in the Bible.

> Happy is the man who finds wisdom,
> And the man who gains understanding;
> For her proceeds are better than the profits of silver,
> And her gain than fine gold.
> She is more precious than rubies,
> And all the things you may desire cannot compare
>   with her.
> Length of days is in her right hand,
> In her left hand riches and honor.
> Her ways are ways of pleasantness,
> And all her paths are peace.
> She is a tree of life to those who take hold of her,
> And happy are all who retain her. (Proverbs 3:13–18 NKJV)

If we held on to wisdom like this, growing old would be like taking hold of a great treasure. If we could open ourselves to this wisdom that comes from God, we would be truly rich and extremely wealthy in the ways that matter most. But not all wisdom comes from God.

> Do not be wise in your own eyes;
> Fear the LORD and depart from evil.
> It will be health to your flesh,
> And strength to your bones. (Proverbs 3:7–8 NKJV)

Wait, what? First of all, there is a wisdom we shouldn't desire. And, shocker, it's our *own* wisdom. These verses tell us we should shoo away our own wisdom, depart from evil, and fear the Lord.

But here's the wild part. Doing this will bring health to our flesh and strength to our bones! This is the kind of youthful glow and strength and power that is to be desired, even as we age.

Wow, thank You, God, for giving us the key to true health and strength.

As we dig deeper into Scripture, we see that many of the people God used in powerful and significant ways in the Bible began their most influential works when they were advanced in years. Moses, Abraham, Noah—so many of these epic people were eighty-plus when they began being used by God in significant ways.

We can also see this in more recent history. John Pemberton invented Coca-Cola at age fifty-five. John Glenn went to space at age seventy-seven.[2] Noah Webster completed his *American Dictionary of the English Language* at age sixty-six. Peter Roget

IF WE OPEN OURSELVES UP TO GOD'S WISDOM, WE WILL BE RICH IN THE WAYS THAT MATTER MOST.

invented the thesaurus at age seventy-three.[3] Colonel Sanders started KFC at age sixty-five.[4] Benjamin Franklin signed the Declaration of Independence at age seventy.[5] Ronald Reagan entered politics at age fifty-four.[6] And Nelson Mandela was elected president of South Africa at age seventy-five.[7]

So don't let anyone tell you that you can't do things for God and for this world when you're old; it's something not to be dreaded but embraced. Being "full of years" is only a bad thing if they are bad years—so make them good! I pray that reading this would inspire you and give you hope for the years to come in your life and in your marriage, no matter how many years are behind you and ahead of you. God has only just begun in your heart and in your life and in your marriage.

Let's not focus on keeping a tight grip on our physical youth as we get older. Let's see past the veneer into the depth of trusting Jesus and fearing the Lord. Let's keep ourselves in the love of God, walking with Him and letting His wisdom be health to our flesh and strength to our bones. We can become more beautiful and handsomer the older we get because of the beauty and power that is within us—in our souls. That doesn't mean we won't face the realities of age as we grow old together, but we will be confident and stronger and better in that season. Let it be, Lord!

BRING IT HOME

- If time is making you more of what you are in your relationship, what's it making you into now? What would you like it to make you into as you get on in years?
- Is there a couple in your life you know who wear (or wore) their

golden years well, like a crown of glory? What about them do you admire and want to emulate?

- Do you envision things getting more boring for you as you get older, or more fun and exciting? How can you reframe aging as a good thing in your mind?

CONVERSATION STARTERS

- "When I envision growing old with you, I look forward to _____. I worry about _____."
- "When we first met, the thing I used to dream about my future with you was _____. Now, that thing is _____."
- "As we age, I want to become more of what we are now in the area of _____. I want to invest more in the area of _____."

PRAYER

Thank You, God, for the passing of time and for the gaining of wisdom and discernment. Give us the eyes to see and the strength to take hold of the wisdom You will use like the fountain of youth in our hearts and marriage. We want all the gray hairs on our heads to be a reflection of the righteousness and wisdom that come from a lifetime of following You. Let us welcome growing old together and plant seeds now that will grow into something glorious over time. You are so good, Lord. In Jesus' name, amen.

When they saw the boldness of Peter and John, and perceived that they were uneducated, common men, they were astonished. And they recognized that they had been with Jesus.

ACTS 4:13 ESV

CHAPTER 52

UPWARD, FORWARD, ONWARD

JENNIE

I n Mark 3 we read about a time when Jesus was in a synagogue, and there was a man there who had a withered hand. The Bible says the religious leaders watched Jesus closely. Seeing Jesus and then seeing the man with a broken hand, they knew that Jesus was going to try something. So instead of watching Jesus in wonder and anticipation and excitement for something unexpected He would do, they watched Him to catch Him doing something wrong. It was the Sabbath, and no one could work on the Sabbath—no one except for God. These guys had been trying to catch Jesus breaking the law. I wonder if they planted the man with the withered hand in the front row, waiting to see what Jesus would do.

The sad thing to me is that these men had a front-row seat to Jesus Christ. Whenever Jesus was speaking or healing or walking or living, they saw Him. They saw Him, but they missed Him. They got to see what we only wish we could've seen and experienced, but they were blind. This shows that proximity to Jesus doesn't mean a changed life or a saved soul. It's possible to be in church and say we're a Christian but not know Jesus as our Lord and our Savior. These were the religious leaders! It's possible to be a leader who is religious, to be a leader or a pastor of a church, and not see Jesus for who He is. *Lord, let it be far from us that we would be immersed in the church but not lovers of Jesus, with eyes to see Him and hearts to obey Him.*

What would you do if you had a front-row seat to Jesus' life and miracles and messages?

I think I would just sit there, eyes wide open—probably mouth wide open. I think I would watch His every move, hang on to every word, and just listen. I don't know if I would even have the right questions. These religious leaders were six feet away from God in the flesh, and they were blind to His majesty and royalty and beauty. I don't know a lot of things, but I do know that to be near Jesus, but not *with* Him and in love with Him, is a dangerous place to be.

I pray that it wouldn't be so with us. That we would see Jesus with all our hearts and souls and minds and beings. That we would watch Him closely, hanging on every word He says, letting His words set the pace for our lives and our marriages, and keeping us steady as we go.

Today's verse is found in Acts 4. In the previous chapter of Acts, Peter and John had healed a disabled man who had been that way since birth. The people who saw it were amazed, and Peter seized the moment to preach the gospel, sharing the bad news of their sin and the good news of Jesus Christ, the only name that saves. He told them, "Repent therefore and be converted, that your sins may be blotted out, so that times of refreshing may come from the presence of the Lord" (Acts 3:19 NKJV).

Guess who was mad about this? Exactly—the priests, the captain of the temple, and the Sadducees, the religious leaders. Acts 4:2 says they were "greatly disturbed that [the apostles] taught the people and preached in Jesus the resurrection from the dead" (NKJV). So they put Peter and John in prison.

I just want to add here that we have to fight against a religious spirit. It's in all of us to some extent. A religious and pharisaic vibe is easy—cutting down, criticizing, thinking our way is the only way and everyone else is barbaric and wrong and sinful and bad. We have got to fight this tendency and choose faith, belief, and truth instead.

The reality is, God will still work and move in only the way He can even when we try to stop it. Verse 4 says that about five thousand men believed that day. Instead of fighting a fresh work that God might want to use, let's have faith to see that God could use anything and anyone.

Our verse today tells us that when the religious leaders "saw the boldness of Peter and John, and perceived that they were uneducated, common men, they were astonished. And they *recognized that they had been with Jesus*" (esv). It was obvious that Peter and John were just regular guys who hadn't had any training, but the religious leaders also saw that these men had spent time with Jesus. Wow.

This is just the kind of thing God delights in doing. He loves doing a beautiful work through unexpected situations and people. He gets the glory, and people come to know Him. Sometimes it's wild and sometimes it's weird, but God loves to choose the foolish things of the world, to shame those who think they know everything (1 Corinthians 1:27).

You two might wonder what God has in store for you. You might look at the next five years and see a lot of question marks and empty space. I want to remind you that regardless of your training or education, regardless of how foolish you might feel or your situation might be, God chooses you and wants to use you and your marriage. The most important thing about you is whose you are, that you are God's son and His daughter. And time spent in His presence will never be a waste. Time with Jesus will always

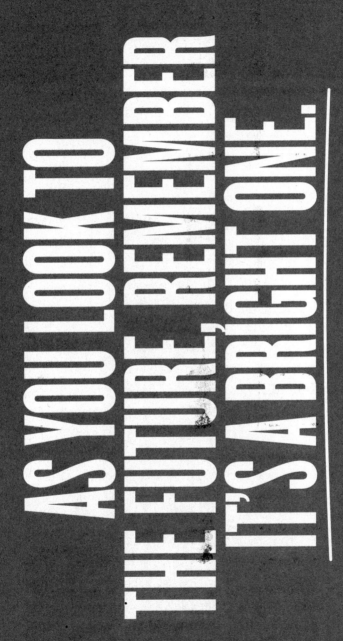

AS YOU LOOK TO THE FUTURE, REMEMBER, IT'S A BRIGHT ONE.

NOT BECAUSE OF YOU, BUT BECAUSE OF JESUS IN YOU.

change your life and transform your mind and heart. Real times of refreshing come only from the presence of the Lord.

Our prayer for you is that your future will be full and flourishing and that the windows of heaven might be opened so that God can pour out a blessing on you, and that dreams you never thought you could see fulfilled will happen in your marriage because you've been with Jesus. And not just looked at Jesus or noticed Him, not just heard about Him, not just gone through a devotional, but you've been *with* Him and pursued Him together.

God has so much for you. And He has so much *more* for you. As we get excited and anticipate what He is going to do in five years, in ten years, in five months, in five minutes even, we believe that He's going to do "exceedingly abundantly above all that we ask or think" (Ephesians 3:20 NKJV)—even in (and especially in) the hard stuff we walk through.

As you look to the future, remember it's a bright one, not because of you but because of Jesus in you. As you keep Jesus at the center of your marriage, as you fight for honor, as you love, respect, and pursue your better half, God will show up in unexpected ways. He will fight for you. He honors those who honor Him.

This marriage you are in is beautiful right now. God sees you right where you are, and while there is struggle and pain, the mess is part of the process. The struggle is making you stronger. The struggle is proof that you're still fighting and you have successfully not given up. Lean into the discomfort, to the conflict, to the hard things, and see God bring power where there was pain. A microphone where there was mess. Joy where there was numbness. As you do the work, in five years you will look back and see Him and His faithfulness. And you will have fresh eyes for each other. You will see a depth and beauty in your relationship that you never thought possible. This is the abundant life Jesus came to give us. It's now. Don't miss the little moments; be present, right here, right now.

We are so honored to have had this time with you, and we are so excited for what God has for you as you walk in His love together. Go get 'em!

BRING IT HOME

- When have you felt the difference between just looking at and seeing Jesus, and truly knowing and following Him? What did that shift look like?
- Of all the advice and guidance and marriage strategy you've gathered from going through this book, what seems the most daunting? How does it make you feel to know that a close relationship with Jesus is the only thing that makes these things work?
- Where in your marriage do you most hope to invite in Jesus' supernatural power to change and transform?

YOUR FIVE-YEAR PLAN

After everything you've discovered and been through together in this process, sit down with your notes and discuss your hopes for the next five years.

- What wisdom do you hope to apply?
- What changes will you implement?

- What adventures do you want to go on?
- What do you want to create?
- How do you want to serve?
- What do you want to enjoy?
- Who do you hope to be together as a couple?
- What difference do you hope to bring to the world?
- How do you pray that God will grow you?
- What will you keep in your back pocket as you proceed with caution down marriage roads that you know are dangerous and slippery?

Be bold, be brave, and maintain a prayerful closeness to Jesus in this process. As you have been with Him, His power, hope, and stability will begin to appear in your future.

PRAYER

Lord God, You are holy. You are just. You are good. And we just sit in this moment, taking in all You have been bringing to our relationship. You have healed, You have mended, You have moved—and we say thank You. Lord, You are also the Way forward. And wherever You call us, we trust You. We seek You first, knowing that You will take care of all things as we follow You with our whole hearts in this marriage You have given us. We pray for greater depth, greater empathy, greater fun, and greater sex. We love You! In Jesus' name, amen.

SUPERPOWERED

When we started this journey with you, we let you in on a moment we could have (and maybe should have) kept to ourselves and not shared. To fall while riding a bike is humiliating. I (Jennie) remember when I was first learning to road bike. I had clipped my shoes into the pedals, and when Levi and I stopped at a stoplight, I didn't unclip in time. I literally fell fully over, and scraped up my knee, but it was my pride that hurt the most.

On that slippery day in Chicago, it was the same thing, but because I was mad at Levi, it all hurt even more.

We know that some moments are more humiliating than others and we know that vulnerability can be hard, but we hope in our journey together that you saw the beauty of letting down your guard and humbling yourself, and maybe even laughing at yourself a little.

We want to end by reminding you that you don't have to ride your bikes mad anymore. You don't have to try and make your marriage work and be happy and strong in your own strength. That will never help you, and it will usually end with falling hard and getting hurt.

These days, our favorite kind of bikes to ride are our e-bikes. (It's probably a being-forty thing, but we are more than okay with that.) We can still pedal if we want to, but the pedaling enables the machine of the bike to engage, and we can go faster and farther *and* it's really fun.

Think of your marriage now with the power of the Holy Spirit propelling you forward instead of your own strength. He is your power source; He will keep you going when you're weak and tired and can't muster up anything to bring to your marriage.

With this in mind, we want to bless you as you go. You two are special. You are so loved by God, and He delights in you. Your relationship is unique. He has so much more for you individually and together. He has called you to live with confidence, strength, kindness, tenderness, and joy. When you feel like you've hit a wall, don't disengage, but stay steady. Stay on your toes, ready to listen for His voice, ready to keep walking and obeying, ready to serve and honor your spouse, especially when they're not doing their part.

We pray for grace to mark your life. That there would be a shift in the building of your relationship, that you would see the struggle and the hard stuff you walk through as the foundation being built stronger and the inner strength of your marriage deepening.

You two are meant to go the distance, to run this race well and together. Run hard, rest well, refresh each other, keep focusing on Jesus, and you'll be unstoppable and unslippable. Let's ride.

Levi & Jennie

ACKNOWLEDGMENTS

t's hard to know where to start. We feel spoiled to be surrounded by so many beautiful couples who have led the way in both victory and in mistakes, in honor and in fun, in joy and in grief.

Skip and Lenya Heitzig, thank you for showing us what commitment looks like, for being there for us during dark days, and for showing us what it looks like to love unconditionally and to laugh.

Greg and Cathe Laurie, thank you for living out faithfulness in marriage and in ministry, and demonstrating what it looks like to grieve together as a couple.

Louie and Shelley Giglio, thank you for showing us what it looks like to be passionate about what God wants in our lives, to run and risk, and also to rest. You've shown us what it looks like to bring people in and how to love people like they were your own. You also are just fun.

Thank you Alivia, our firstborn, who has watched firsthand, in the front row, the good, the bad, and the ugly in our marriage. Thank you specifically for helping watch the kids while we needed to write, or have a "meeting," whether that meant an actual meeting or a pretend one so we could make out.

Thank you, Elisha, for designing this stunning cover and the inside art, and for your input; it's always helpful. Thank you, Ryan, for working so hard on the cover design we originally wanted when the book was titled *Slippery When Wet*.

ACKNOWLEDGMENTS

Thank you, Katelyn, for your sweet, encouraging spirit, and for your help, insight, and hard work.

Dear children and future grandchildren and great-grandchild and beyond, we love you, and we're here for you and believe in you. Maybe this book will help you and encourage you in your marriages.

You are so special to us, and we will fight for you and be in your corner all our days, on into eternity.

NOTES

CHAPTER 1: RIGHT PLACE, RIGHT TIME

1. Corrie ten Boom, *Each New Day: 365 Reflections to Strengthen Your Faith*, repackaged ed. (1977; 2003; Grand Rapids: Revell Company, 2013), 78.

CHAPTER 3: MARRIAGE: THE ROLE OF A LIFETIME

1. G. M. Landes, *Building Your Biblical Hebrew Vocabulary: Learning Words by Frequency and Cognate*, 2nd ed. (Atlanta: Society of Biblical Literature, 2001), 137.

CHAPTER 4: PRACTICE HIS PRESENCE

1. "Internet Trends 2022: Stats & Facts in the U.S. and Worldwide," vpnMentor, accessed April 27, 2022, https://www.vpnmentor.com/blog/vital-internet-trends/.

2. Julia Naftulin, "Here's How Many Times We Touch Our Phones Every Day," Business Insider, July 13, 2016, https://www.business insider.com/dscout-research-people-touch-cell-phones-2617-times-a-day-2016-7.

3. Oliver Holden, "Secret Prayer," *The Young Convert's Companion, Being a Collection of Hymns for the Use of Conference Meetings* (Boston: E. Lincoln, 1806; repr. in Charles S. Sutter and Wilbur F. Tillett, *The Hymns and Hymn Writers of the Church: An Annotated Edition of the Methodist Hymnal* [New York: Eaton & Mains, 1911]), 272.

4. Allen C. Myers, ed., *The Eerdmans Bible Dictionary* (Grand Rapids: Eerdmans, 1987), 215.

CHAPTER 5: A MARRIAGE THAT WORKS

1. Steven Spielberg, interview by Lesley Stahl, *60 Minutes*, October 21, 2012, https://www.cbsnews.com/news/spielberg-a-directors-life-reflected-in-film/.

2. Cal Fussman, "Dr. Dre: What I've Learned," *Esquire*, December 11, 2013, http://www.esquire.com/entertainment /music/news/a23843 /dr-dre-interview-0114/.

CHAPTER 6: BE THE ONE

1. Andy Stanley, *The New Rules for Love, Sex, and Dating* (Grand Rapids: Zondervan, 2014), 50.

CHAPTER 8: GIVE MOSES A PINK SLIP

1. If this is something you want more information about how to enter into, please visit freshlife.church and click on "Know God."

CHAPTER 9: BEEF UP THAT MARRIAGE ACCOUNT

1. Sam Becker, "How Much Money You Could Have If You Invest $1 a Day Starting When Your Child Is Born," Acorns, January 31, 2020, https://grow.acorns.com/what-happens-when-you-invest-one -dollar-a-day-for-your-child/.

CHAPTER 13: PLANT A GARDEN

1. Debbie Walter, "Beware of These 6 Little Foxes," *The Romantic Vineyard* (blog), July 31, 2013, https://theromanticvineyard.com /2013/07/31/bewareofthese6littlefoxes.

2. That's actually the title of a great book for women by Linda Dillow, *What's It Like Being Married to Me?: And Other Dangerous Questions* (Colorado Springs: David C. Cook, 2011). Read it if you dare.

CHAPTER 15: SEX ON OUR MINDS

1. Warren Wiersbe, *Be Skillfull (Proverbs): God's Guidebook to Wise Living*, 2nd ed. (Colorado Springs: David C. Cook, 2009), 62.
2. Dictionary.com, s.v. "let *(v.)*," accessed April 28, 2022, https://www.dictionary.com/browse/let.
3. William D. Mounce, ed., *Mounce's Complete Expository Dictionary of Old & New Testament Words* (Grand Rapids: Zondervan, 2006), 1048.
4. Gary Thomas and Debra Fileta, *Married Sex: A Christian Couple's Guide to Reimagining Your Sex Life* (Grand Rapids: Zondervan, 2021), 5.
5. Richard Whitaker, ed., *The Abridged Brown-Driver-Briggs Hebrew-English Lexicon of the Old Testament* (Boston: Houghton Mifflin, 1906).

CHAPTER 16: BUILDING A FIRE

1. Associated Press, "Stradivarius Violin Sold for $16 million," NBC News, June 21, 2011, https://www.nbcnews.com/id/wbna43478088.
2. If not, find out your spouse's love language! You can both take a quiz at https://www.5lovelanguages.com/.

CHAPTER 17: BRINGING SEXY BACK

1. C. S. Lewis, *The Weight of Glory: And Other Addresses* (1949; repr., New York: HarperOne, 2001), 47.

CHAPTER 18: LOOK UP, CHILD

1. Neil deGrasse Tyson, interview by Charlie Rose, *60 Minutes*, March 22, 2015, https://www.cbsnews.com/news/neil-degrasse-tyson-astrophysicist-charlie-rose-60-minutes-2.
2. *The ESV Study Bible* (Wheaton, IL: Crossway, 2008), 1858.

CHAPTER 21: ROGAINE FOR YOUR SOUL

1. Leland Ryken, James C. Wilhoit, Tremper Longman III, eds., *Dictionary of Biblical Imagery* (Downers Grove, IL: IVP Academic, 1998), s.v. "seven."

CHAPTER 22: STAY HUMBLE AND SHOW HONOR

1. Lewis defined this term as "the uncritical acceptance of the intellectual climate of our own age and the assumption that whatever has gone out of date is on that count discredited" in C. S. Lewis, *Surprised by Joy* (San Diego: Harcourt Brace Jovanovich, 1966), 207.

CHAPTER 25: HOW TO SPELL *HUMILITY*, PART 2

1. Daniel Jones, "The 36 Questions That Lead to Love," *New York Times*, January 9, 2015, https://www.nytimes.com/2015/01/09/style/no-37-big-wedding-or-small.html.

2. Stephanie Kirby, "25 Questions to Help You Get to Know Someone Deeply," BetterHelp, last updated April 1, 2022, https://www.betterhelp.com/advice/relations/25-questions-to-get-to-know-someone-deeply.

CHAPTER 29: HEART TENDERIZER

1. James Strong, *A Concise Dictionary of the Words in the Greek Testament and the Hebrew Bible* (Bellingham, WA: Faithlife: 2009), 68, via Logos Bible Software.

CHAPTER 31: LUCKY IN LOVE

1. Winn Collier, *A Burning in My Bones: The Authorized Biography of Eugene H. Peterson, Translator of the Message* (Colorado Springs: Waterbrook, 2021), 219–20.

2. Editorial Staff, "Unhappy Marriage Can Get Happier," Divorce Source, May 10, 2016, https://www.divorcesource.com/blog/unhappy-marriages-can-get-happier.

CHAPTER 32: AS FOR ME

1. Linda Dillow, *What's It Like to Be Married to Me?: And Other Dangerous Questions* (Colorado Springs: David C. Cook, 2011).

2. Holly Furtick, *Becoming Mrs. Betterhalf* (Matthews, NC: Elevation

Church, 2016), available at https://store.elevationchurch.org /products/becoming-mrs-betterhalf-digital-workbook.

CHAPTER 33: SOUL TRAINING

1. Eugene H. Peterson, *A Long Obedience in the Same Direction: Discipleship in an Instant Society* (Downers Grove, IL: IVP, 1980).
2. Theresa E. DiDonato, "5 Reasons Why Couples Who Sweat Together, Stay Together," *Psychology Today*, January 10, 2014, https://www.psychologytoday.com/gb/blog/meet-catch-and-keep /201401/5-reasons-why-couples-who-sweat-together-stay-together.

CHAPTER 35: MONEY MATTERS

1. Catey Hill, "This Common Behavior Is the No. 1 Predictor of Whether You'll Get Divorced," MarketWatch, January 10, 2018, https://www.marketwatch.com/story/this-common-behavior-is-the -no-1-predictor-of-whether-youll-get-divorced-2018–01–10.
2. For more information about Financial Peace University, see https:// www.ramseysolutions.com/ramseyplus/financial-peace.
3. Rachel Cruze, *Know Yourself, Know Your Money* (Franklin, TN: Ramsey Press, 2021).

CHAPTER 36: THE GENEROUS LIFE

1. Bible Hub, s.v. "1293. berakah," Brown-Driver-Briggs, accessed August 11, 2022, https://biblehub.com/hebrew/1293.htm.
2. The Free Dictionary, s.v. "generous," accessed April 30, 2022, https://www.thefreedictionary.com/generous.
3. Gary Chapman, *The Five Love Languages: How to Express Heartfelt Commitment to Your Mate* (Chicago: Northfield, 1992).
4. Gary Chapman, *The Four Seasons of Marriage: Secrets to a Lasting Marriage* (Carol Stream, IL: Tyndale, 2005).

CHAPTER 38: IN THE SAME WAY

1. Warren W. Wiersbe, *Be Hopeful (1 Peter): How to Make the Best of*

Times Out of Your Worst of Times (Colorado Springs: David C. Cook, 2010), 80.

CHAPTER 39: THE *S* WORDS

1. Strong's Concordance, s.v. "hupotassó,"Bible Hub, accessed April 30, 2022, https://biblehub.com/greek/5293.htm.

CHAPTER 42: YOU ARE SEEN

1. Katherine Wolf and Jay Wolf, *Hope Heals: A True Story of Overwhelming Loss and an Overcoming Love* (Grand Rapids: Zondervan, 2016), 145.

CHAPTER 43: THE SIGNIFICANCE OF YOUR OTHER

1. "Plant Nutrients in the Soil | 17 Growth Elements," *AgriTutorials*, September 5, 2020, https://agritutorials.com/plant-nutrients-in-the-soil/.
2. Matthew Henry, *Matthew Henry's Commentary on the Bible*, Genesis 2:21–25, accessed May 1, 2022, https://www.biblegateway.com/resources/matthew-henry/Gen.2.21-Gen.2.25.
3. Shyamala Iyer, "Atoms and Life," Arizona State University: Ask a Biologist, September 27, 2009, https://askabiologist.asu.edu/content/atoms-life.

CHAPTER 44: CHOOSE TO SEE THE GOOD

1. Mark A. Lamport, ed., *Encyclopedia of Martin Luther and the Reformation* (Lanham, MD: Rowman & Littlefield, 2017), 264.

CHAPTER 45: THE GENERATIONS

1. Aimee Picchi, "Modern Families: Multigenerational Households Are on the Rise, Thanks to Financial and Emotional Benefits," *USA Today*, July 16, 2020, https://eu.usatoday.com/story/money/columnist/2020/07/16/multigenerational-households-rise-prepare-pros-and-cons/5447028002/.

CHAPTER 50: YOU IN FIVE YEARS

1. Katherine Wolf and Jay Wolf, *Hope Heals: A True Story of Overwhelming Loss and an Overcoming Love* (Grand Rapids: Zondervan, 2016), 137.

CHAPTER 51: I WANNA GROW OLD WITH YOU

1. "More Than Half of Americans Want to Live to 100 but Worry About Affording Longer Lifespans," Business Wire, April 10, 2019, https://www.businesswire.com/news/home/20190410005283/en/Americans-Live-100-Worry-Affording-Longer-Lifespans.

2. Dan Waldschmidt, "This List Proves You're Never Too Old to Do Something Amazing," Business Insider, March 13, 2014, https://www.businessinsider.com/100-amazing-accomplishments-achieved-at-every-age-2014-3.

3. Jesse Birnbaum, "Satisfying Verbomania," *TIME*, September 7, 1992, https://content.time.com/time/subscriber/article/0,33009,976432,00.html.

4. Chris Plante, "The Real Story of Colonel Sanders Is Far Crazier Than This Bland Inspirational Meme," The Verge, July 5, 2016, https://www.theverge.com/2016/7/5/12096466/colonel-sanders-kfc-meme-life-story.

5. Alyson Shontell, "Many Founding Fathers Were Shockingly Young When the Declaration of Independence Was Signed in 1776," Business Insider, July 5, 2014, https://www.businessinsider.com/age-of-founding-fathers-on-july-4-1776-2014-7.

6. "Reagan's Pre-Presidential Biographical Sketch and Timeline, 1911–1980," Ronald Reagan Presidential Library and Museum, accessed May 1, 2022, https://www.reaganlibrary.gov/reagans/ronald-reagan/reagans-pre-presidential-biographical-sketch-timeline-1911–1980.

7. Vera Songwe, "The Mandela Rule—A Legacy to African Leaders," Brookings, December 6, 2013, https://www.brookings.edu/blog/africa-in-focus/2013/12/06/the-mandela-rule-a-legacy-to-african-leaders/.

ABOUT THE AUTHORS

L evi and Jennie Lusko pioneered Fresh Life Church in 2007. The ministry includes locations in Montana, Utah, Oregon, Idaho, Wyoming, and reaches around the world online. Levi and Jennie have one son: Lennox, and four daughters: Alivia, Daisy, Clover, and Lenya, who is in heaven. Jennie is the bestselling author of *The Fight to Flourish*. Levi is the bestselling author of several books, including *Through the Eyes of a Lion*, *I Declare War*, and *The Last Supper on the Moon*. They host a podcast together called *Hey! It's the Luskos* and can be found on summer evenings riding their bikes to get Mexican food.

ROAR LIKE A LION

With eye-catching art, fascinating stories and fun facts, Bible verses and prayers, and simple action steps, this ninety-day devotional will help your kids approach both fun moments and tough times with their hearts set on God's faithfulness.

Roar Like a Lion covers highly relevant topics such as:

- Facing fears about school and friendships

- Dealing with peer pressure and bullying

- Handling new challenges, disappointments, and grief

- Having courage to try something new

- Understanding how we each fit into God's great story

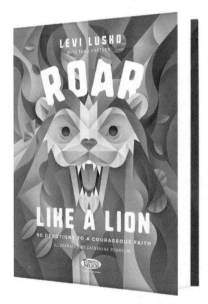

Download a free accompanying parent guide at roarlikealionbook.com/parentguide.

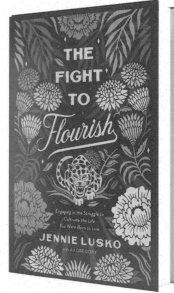